Dan O'Bannon sees a story as a battles. His is a dynamic and pr will help you in the often-exaspe ...g process of story creating, which is the writer's constant dilemma.

— Professor David Howard, Screenwriting Division University of Southern California School of Cinematic Arts

Ingeniously literate, charmingly irreverent, and terrifically entertaining, *Dan O'Bannon's Guide to Screenplay Structure* is as original as the great screenwriter himself. It's a fascinating peek into the mind of one of the masters of the fantasy film and an incisive work of criticism.

— Jason Zinoman, arts critic, *New York Times*; author, *Shock Value: How a Few Eccentric Outsiders Invented Modern Horror*

How does a natural storyteller talk about storytelling? Well, he makes a story of it – and that's exactly what the great Dan O'Bannon does in his *Guide to Screenplay Structure*. The book is smart and smart-assed, cantankerous and cagey, illuminating and endlessly entertaining – the rare how-to manual you can read straight through for the sheer pleasure of it.

— Sam Hamm, screenwriter, *Batman*, *Monkeybone*, *Never Cry Wolf*

Sometimes angry, often funny, always insightful, *Dan O'Bannon's Guide to Screenplay Structure* is a clear and engaging examination of story craft written by someone who has not merely studied the subject but has also lived it.

— Richard Walter, professor, UCLA Screenwriting Chairman

A treasure trove of secrets to writing great screenplays by a true master. Clear, concise, and inspirational (as well as great fun), this book allows us to learn from the great Dan O'Bannon himself who, unlike other 'how-to' writers, has actually created screenplays that have become cinema classics.

— Stuart Gordon, director, co-writer, *Re-Animator*

This superb book is filled with original and practical exercises that will benefit the beginner and seasoned veteran alike. Dan's love of writing and reverence for writers – as well as his humanity – are in evidence on every page.

> — Jeffrey Davis, chair, Screenwriting Department, School of Film and Television, Loyola Marymount University

Read it before you type another word!

> — Catherine Clinch columnist, *Media Grazing at Film News Briefs*; writer, *Hart to Hart*, *The Love Boat*, *Hunter*

A straight-shooting, unsentimental antidote to every feel-good, hand-holding screenwriting book on the shelf.

> — Webster Stone, executive producer, *The Conspirator*, *Gone in 60 Seconds*, *The Negotiator*

A readable, thoughtful, and über-thorough look at the complex process of writing an effective screenplay, complete with exercises that task the reader to analyze his or her own writing. Great examples, ranging from Aristotle's *Poetics* to *Alien*.

> — Barbara Doyle, chair, film division, Dodge College of Film and Media Arts, Chapman University

As fun to read as one of his screenplays, as idiosyncratic and smart as the working of this artist's brilliant mind.

> — Nick Castle, writer/director, *August Rush*, *Hook*, *The Boy Who Could Fly*, *Tap*, *The Last Starfighter*

Dan O'Bannon made movies worth watching, and his *Guide to Screenplay Structure* is a superior lesson in how to start things off right by building a more exciting structure for your script. Any screenwriting book that uses Aristotle to analyze *The Texas Chain Saw Massacre* is a must-read.

> — Blair Davis, assistant professor, media and cinema studies, DePaul University

How pleasant to read a screenwriting book by someone who has actually written great screenplays. Dan O'Bannon's insights and analysis make you want to throw all other screenplay manuals in the trash.

> — Larry Karaszewski, Golden Globe–winning writer, *Ed Wood*, *The People vs. Larry Flynt*, *Percy Jackson: Sea of Monsters*

This will be the definitive book for anyone who dreams of writing a successful script for movies. A must-have book for all future and current filmmakers, writers and directors.

> — Mark L. Lester, director, *Firestarter*, *Commando*, *Class of 1984*

What you hold in your hand is not just another book on how to muddle your way through writing a screenplay. It is a course on screenwriting and the intricacies that go into writing for the screen, taught by a true industry professional. The ins and outs of structure, conflict and character are all laid out before you. Not just the 'what to do' but the 'why' and the 'how' to do it."

> — Duppy Demetrius, writer, *24*, *The Closer*, *Major Crimes*

Dan O'Bannon's personal observations on his work and his process are insightful and inspiring. He made me analyze not just his approach, but my own. At times, I felt as if I were in a room having a conversation with a fellow writer.

> — Reggie Rock Bythewood, writer/director, *Get on the Bus*, *Biker Boyz*, *Notorious*

Written in a style that carefully blends the personal and the professional, *Dan O'Bannon's Guide to Screenplay Structure* is more than a book. It is like an opportunity to sit down with a Hollywood insider over coffee and get the skinny on what it takes to make it in the business.

> — Dr. Gregory K. Allen, supervising professor, The Sprocket Guild

A successful screenwriter, Dan O'Bannon is more invested in great writing than in obeying rules. At the core of his book are twelve case studies of classic plays and scripts. The book analyzes each work with O'Bannon's story structural system. It shows you how the rules apply and, perhaps equally important, when they don't and why. You can use the book as a workbook, a guide, or a call to excellence. This book can be useful for writers at any level and for scripts at any stage of development.

> — Mildred Lewis, award-winning filmmaker and playwright; cofounder, The Fox Lewis Project

There are three things you must have to be a successful screenwriter — persistence, a good story, and the book you are holding in your hand.

> — Robert A. Nowotny, president, Teocalli Entertainment; creator, NeedToVent.com

Dan O'Bannon's Guide to Screenplay Structure presents a new take on an old subject: movie narrative. Sometimes angry, often funny, always insightful, here is a clear and engaging examination of story craft written by someone who has not merely studied the subject but has lived it. The book explores film classics and also the author's own highly regarded scripts. More than mere analysis, it provides a hands-on practitioner's vantage of interest not only to writers but also to all movie lovers who seek and cherish solid stories.

> — Prof. Richard Walter, UCLA Screenwriting Chairman; author, *Essentials of Screenwriting*

DAN O'BANNON'S

GUIDE TO SCREENPLAY STRUCTURE

by Dan O'Bannon with Matt R. Lohr

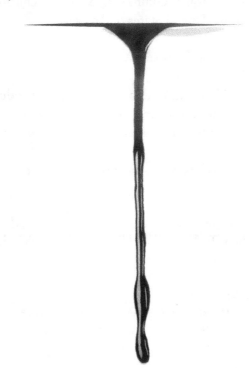

Inside Tips from the Writer of
ALIEN, TOTAL RECALL & THE RETURN OF THE LIVING DEAD

Published by Michael Wiese Productions
12400 Ventura Blvd. #1111
Studio City, CA 91604
tel. 818.379.8799
fax 818.986.3408
mw@mwp.com
www.mwp.com

Cover design: Johnny Ink www.johnnyink.com
Book interior design: Gina Mansfield Design
Editor: Annalisa Zox-Weaver

Printed by McNaughton & Gunn, Inc., Saline, Michigan
Manufactured in the United States of America

Library of Congress Cataloging-in-Publication Data

O'Bannon, Dan.
 Dan O'Bannon's guide to screenplay structure : inside tips from
the writer of Alien, Total recall and Return of the living dead / Dan
O'Bannon ; with Matt R. Lohr.
     p. cm.
 ISBN 978-1-61593-130-9
1. Motion picture authorship. 2. Motion picture authorship-
-Handbooks, manuals, etc. I. Lohr, Matt R., 1978- II. Title. III.
Title: Guide to screeplay structure.
 PN1996.O25 2013
 808.2'3--dc23
                              2012027977

This book is for my dear wife, Diane.

~ DOB

———————

*To Maritsa Darmandzhyan. For better or worse,
this book would not be what it is without her.*

~ MRL

Dynamikos is a Greek word meaning "powerful." "Dynamic" refers to a pattern of growth over time and is characterized by movement, progression, and change.

"Dynamic structure" is my term for stories that are built around the progressive escalation of a conflict.

TABLE OF CONTENTS

FOREWORD
by Roger Corman

———————◆———————

ARTIST, ORIGINATOR, SCREENWRITING MAESTRO.

Few people in this industry managed to surprise and impress me as much as Dan O'Bannon. I was first on his list to produce the picture that would eventually become one of the greatest films of all time: the science fiction masterpiece *Alien*. When he sent me the script, I loved it and immediately wanted to bring its pages to life. Although it obviously did not continue with my involvement, the project proved to me beyond a doubt that Dan was evolving into a rare gem of the motion picture industry.

You might think that someone who possessed the nuts and bolts of that rare quality would want to keep them shrouded in secret, but Dan delivers an exceptionally clear view in this screenwriting guide. Dan not only offers his personal tips and strategies, but he also provides exercises to help you apply the material to your own projects, along with analysis of how other writers might have applied screenwriting structure to their own successful endeavors. His lessons touch upon the past teachings of storytellers like Aristotle and Egri and of modern gurus such as Syd Field and Robert McKee to further demystify the writing process. With his book, Dan places himself high among this first-rate group of teachers.

There is a unique sense of passion and jovial dexterity present in Dan's timeless body of work. You now hold the key to the boundless imagination of a cinematic architect and can study how to structure your own creative thoughts into a screenplay. Dan may be gone, but his words remain and are inscribed here to inspire and educate the next great generation of filmmakers.

Roger Corman

Producer/Director

PREFACE
by Matt R. Lohr

ANY FAN OF SCIENCE FICTION and horror cinema
owes a tip of the cap to Dan O'Bannon. As a director, actor,
visual effects artist, and screenwriter, he was a major mind behind some of the most enduring genre cinema of the last forty
years. He is perhaps best known as the coscenarist (with
Ronald Shusett) and screenwriter of *Alien*, the 1979 classic that took the haunted house picture into deep space and
created an iconic alien monster (kudos to H. R. Giger's stu-
pendous creature designs) that has endured through three sequels, two *Alien Vs. Predator* spin-off pictures, comic books,
toys — you name it. (*Alien* itself now has a permanent home in
the Library of Congress's National Film Registry.) O'Bannon
and Shusett were also credited as coscenarists and screenwriters on 1990's *Total Recall*, the mind-trip sci-fi actioner that gave
Arnold Schwarzenegger one of the best roles of his career. In
addition, O'Bannon cowrote the underrated high-tech helicop-
ter action flick *Blue Thunder* (1983), and he was the writer and
director of 1985's *The Return of the Living Dead*, a splatsticky
horror bash that married zombies and comedy in a way that
presaged such modern genre delights as *Shaun of the Dead*
and *Zombieland*. It all began, of course, with *Dark Star* (1974),
John Carpenter's debut feature as a director, which O'Bannon
cowrote with Carpenter, and in which he played the indelible
role of Sgt. Pinback, who spends much of the film chasing a
beach-ball-bodied alien and who has a memorably hilarious

psychotic breakdown captured on time-lapse videotape. (Incidentally, he was also an editor and production designer on this low-budget feature.) All of these things make Dan O'Bannon essential to any discussion of major genre filmmakers of the last half century. But, to me, Dan was also a friend, a mentor, and an inspiration at a time when my own still-burgeoning career needed it most.

In 2001, I was a student in the graduate screenwriting program at Chapman University in Orange, CA. I had just begun my thesis script under the tutelage of the late Leonard Schrader (an Oscar nominee for his screenplay for *Kiss of the Spider Woman*). During one of our first classes, Leonard mentioned that the school's current "filmmaker-in-residence" was working on a how-to screenwriting book and was looking for a grad student to assist him with editing and polishing the manuscript, and to do some additional writing for the book, including film analyses. During a break, a number of my classmates, wholly independent of one another, came to me and said, "You gotta do this, man. This is all you." When we reconvened, I told Leonard that I would be interested in pursuing this position, and he told me that he'd provide the contact info for the filmmaker-in-residence the next time our class met. You can probably guess by now who that filmmaker was, and that the book he was working on is the one you're now reading.

Working with Dan was not going to be easy for me. He lived in Los Angeles, I was in Orange County — and I did not own an automobile. Every time we met face-to-face over the course of my work for him, I had to rent a car and drive from the O. C. to his home, first in Pacific Palisades and later in Mar Vista, a suburban enclave west of Culver City. The first time we got together, I arrived around noon to find him just wrapping up a viewing of *Law & Order* on A & E. About two minutes into our first conversation, Dan asked me if I'd ever taken psychedelic drugs.

I told him I hadn't. He smirked, looked me up and down, and said, "I didn't think so. You look like Clark Kent." And it's nice to meet *you*, sir.

Something memorable took place every time Dan and I got together to work on the book. One time, he showed me the mounted broadswords hung on the wall of his office. He also let me take a look at several prints of Sir John Tenniel's artwork from *Alice's Adventures in Wonderland*; they were limited edition pressings from the original engraving blocks and had cost him a pretty penny, but Dan said he couldn't resist having them. My favorite day with Dan was when I dropped by to discuss Robert Wise's *The Set-Up* (1949), a film noir centered around the world of boxing, which is discussed briefly in this book. When I arrived, he was just putting a videotape in the old VHS player in his study/office... but it wasn't *The Set-Up*. MGM was preparing to release a special edition DVD of *The Return of the Living Dead*, and they had sent Dan a VHS copy of the film so he could check and approve the digital remastering and color-correction work they had done on the print. "You wanna check some of this out with me?" he asked. And so, as we watched *Return*, I was basically treated to a live director's commentary track, with Dan spinning colorful anecdotes about the production, the actors with whom he had worked and, of course, the film's legendary "split dog" special effect.

And naturally, we talked movies. Dan was a product of the 1970s, arguably Hollywood's golden age of artistic freedom, marooned in a field now run by businessmen and bean counters, and he was never afraid to excoriate the average contemporary studio executive's dearth of imagination... or to send a little disapproval in the direction of modern moviegoers for not demanding better from their entertainment. (I remember him once, in imitation of the "typical" contemporary filmgoer, emitting a series of loud cheep-cheeping sounds... a blind baby bird chirping for its daily regurgitated worm mush). This attitude stemmed from the simple fact that Dan was a firm believer in the importance of a soundly structured screenplay, no surprise considering the elegant construction of many of his most famous scripts. As our work, mostly conducted by telephone and e-mail, progressed over the course of several years, I learned a great deal about how a master screenwriter made his stories tick, and he (I hope) came to respect my views of cinema and how his method applied to pictures we both knew very well but hadn't examined closely in such a way before. We were master and student. We were colleagues. And, though we never stated it as such, I like to think we were friends.

I also became close with Dan's son, Adam, and his wife, Diane, with whom I kept in regular contact following the end of my time on Dan's book. We would exchange occasional e-mails to catch up on my own career progress, and on Dan's battles with both the industry and his own always-problematic health. Diane always let me know that she and Dan were both thinking about me and wishing me the best. In the last years of his life, Dan struggled with an increasingly difficult series of ailments linked to Crohn's disease, which he had initially contracted during the shooting of *Dark Star* and that had plagued him on and off ever since. Most of my final communications with him went through Diane as intermediary, as he spent many of his final years in the care of various medical centers.

Dan passed away on December 17, 2009, several hours before the release of *Avatar*, the science fiction epic directed by James Cameron (who delivered his own spin on Dan's most famous characters in 1986's *Aliens*), which, in addition to being the highest grossing motion picture of all time, was also nominated for nine Academy Awards, including Best Picture. It was, in fact, one of two genre films up for the movie industry's most prestigious award that year; the independently produced South African sci-fi action film *District 9*, released in U.S. theaters several months prior to Dan's death, was also a nominee for the Academy's top prize. It's likely that neither of these films would have been able to break through the critical establishment's traditional prejudice toward genre without the groundwork laid by artists like Dan, who took their tales as seriously as those delivered by any furrow-browed art-house auteur. Diane, who never let me be forgotten, invited me to Dan's private memorial service, during which she informed me that she was still working on finding a home for the book that Dan and I had penned together. Now, that book finally has a home — on your bookshelf.

Working with Dan was one of the most singularly illuminating experiences of my creative life. Partnering with Dan, developing this book with him, and finishing the manuscript after his passing have made me the first fortunate beneficiary of all of the wisdom contained within its pages. Every day that I sit down to work on my own scripts, I find myself pondering Dan's lessons, considering his advice, asking myself, "What would Dan do?" While I was completing the final manuscript, I was simultaneously working on a page-one rewrite of an original spec screenplay, and I have no doubt that the finished product was immensely improved by my consideration and application of Dan's concepts and methods.

Dan's influence on my writing begins with this book, but by no means ends here. I will be utilizing his lessons not just in my own screenwriting work, but also in the evaluations and analyses of classic and contemporary films that I present on my blog, "The Movie Zombie," and at Dan O'Bannon Writing Workshops™ that I will be hosting at conferences and pitch festivals throughout the country and internationally. These workshops will provide hands-on instruction in how to utilize Dan's time-tested, hit-making screenwriting methods to create your own potential blockbusters, whether you write studio-style genre pictures, indie fare, or anything between.

So, to all filmmakers, screenwriters, fans of Dan, and lovers of cinema in general, I hope you enjoy reading this book as much as we did writing it, and that its ideas will prove as useful in the creation of your work as they did for Dan in the writing of his classics. And, if you ever think of taking the easy way out, of settling for less as a screenwriter, Dan would have two words for you. . .

CHEEP CHEEP!

Matt R. Lohr

Los Angeles, 2012

Portions of this preface previously appeared on the "Movie Zombie" blog (themoviezombie.blogspot.com) on December 18, 2009. Reprinted by permission from the author.

INTRODUCTION,
or A Fistful of Popcorn

The secret of being a bore is to tell everything.

— Voltaire

WHILE I WAS IN THE PROCESS OF writing this book, a friend of mine asked me, "What exactly is your book about?"

I said, "It's about focusing the audience's attention into a state of hypnotic concentration on the screen, and holding it there for two hours."

In other words… imagine, when the house lights go down, a hypothetical filmgoer raising a fistful of popcorn to his or her mouth. If the writer has done his job well, two hours later, when "The End" appears on the screen, that same handful of popcorn should still be halfway to that still-open mouth….

WRITING THIS BOOK TOOK ME THIRTY-FIVE YEARS. Three and a half decades of tears and sweat, crawling my way up Hollywood's glass wall, learning how to make movies, how to write screenplays that run over audiences like freight trains. That said, this is *not* a "You-Can-Break-Into-Hollywood" book, telling the reader how to get an agent, sell his/her script, pitch, and so forth. Some authors may offer to teach you how to write a script that "sells every time." No script sells every time. But I will tell you how to write a script that *works* every time.

The shelves of bookstores groan under the weight of all the books out there on how to write a screenplay. If I had never written a script and was looking for advice on how to do so, I would be paralyzed by the sheer abundance of options available. These books promise to tell you absolutely *everything* about screenwriting — and then some. Confronted by such a proliferation of potential methods, I wouldn't know where or how to start.

So, step back from all the books, all the software programs, and remember what you already know. Namely, that the great movies are the ones that deliver — somehow, some way — *the unexpected.* Following all of the established rules of screenwriting (if such a thing is even possible, considering how many rules there are) may produce a "perfect" script, but there will be little room left, amidst all the rule abiding, for anything *astonishing.* All of those "helpful" programs out there, those comprehensive, exhaustive guides on how movies have been written in the past, with a rule for every storytelling move a writer might make, will largely teach you how to write screenplays that have already been written. They can cripple you.

The rules embalm screenplays.

So, in the present work, I will do my best to keep things as simple as possible. The core of this book is a *story structural system,* the same one that I use when I write my own scripts. I will provide you with a structural method that is both minimal and immensely powerful, and it contains prescriptive ideas about how you may invest your own screenplays with that power. Don't allow yourself to be deceived by the simplicity of this system. Once you have it down, everything else falls into place. That is the elegant beauty of it.

The structural system offered in this book, although similar in some respects to other systems, is not identical to any of them, for the simple reason that at the time I invented it (after I wrote *Alien*), I had never studied any other system. I didn't even know other systems existed. You can pick through other writing books till the moon turns green before you find my structural method in any of them. It's not there because it's an original creation. It can only be found in print between the covers of this book, and I offer it to you here for the value it may provide in constructing your own scripts. I will, however, take the time to outline other popular and traditional screenplay structuring systems, so that you may have a full arsenal of techniques at your fingertips. Along the way, I'll share some other advice and ideas that are not structural, but that I have found useful over the years.

My primary advice to you is simply to start writing. Have fun. And look for help *only when you know you have a problem.* Remember: They call it "mastering the rules" because you're supposed to be the rules' master… not their slave.

Chapter One

LOOKING FOR THE FORMULA,
or The Quest for the Watchable Sow's Ear

Attention to trifles makes perfection, and perfection is no trifle.

— Michelangelo

I N 1978, WHEN *ALIEN* WAS IN PRODUCTION at 20th
Century-Fox, I decided that it would be handy if I could devise
some sort of formula for writing screenplays. I was looking to
lessen the burden of invention and make it more likely that I
could get all the way to the end of a story without having it
collapse into chaos. Up until that time, it was merely a matter
of luck whether one of my scripts worked all the way through
to the end or eventually lost its narrative thrust and wandered
off track. As long as I felt inspired, the screenplay would work.
When inspiration failed, as it always did at some point, I had no
way to be certain of what I ought to write next, if my ideas were
to the point, or even if the script was boring. A *formula*. That
would guarantee reliable storytelling results every time. Right?

I was imagining some sort of plot-and-character checklist
into which I could plug my story elements. I mentioned this
notion to Gordon Carroll, one of the producers of *Alien*, and
he said, "Oh, well, there is a book that lists every possible type
of plot."

My ears swiveled forward like a cat's. "Really?? What is this
book?"

"I've got it around here somewhere." Gordon dug around
and came up with a musty little volume with a faded blue
cloth cover. *Plotto*, by one William Wallace Cook. Subtitle:
The Master Book of All Plots. Copyright 1928.

This book was just what I was looking for. "Can I borrow this?"

"Go right ahead."

———————— ✦ ————————

"THE PLOTTO METHOD," begins Cook, "enables the Plottoist to begin his story with a Masterplot and marshal his situations or Conflicts in conformity to it; or, it enables him to begin with a situation or Conflict and consciously to watch the particular Theme as the plot unfolds."[1]

Yes. Go on.

"If the main Conflict selected is built around A, or B, alone, the A or B group shall be scanned; if around A and B alone, the A and B group will yield suggestions, or the A or B group may be found to serve…"

Bear in mind: This advice was all in tremendously tiny print. But I wasn't in this for my health.

"Conflicts," continued Cook, "fall into the following general classifications:

Conflicts in Misfortune.
Conflicts in Mistaken Judgment.
Conflicts in Helpfulness.
Conflicts in Deliverance.
Conflicts in Idealism.
Conflicts in Obligation.
Conflicts in Necessity.
Conflicts in Chance.
Conflicts in Personal Limitations.
Conflicts in Simulation.
Conflicts in Craftiness.
Conflicts in Transgression.
Conflicts in Revenge.
Conflicts in Mystery.
Conflicts in Revelation."[2]

[1] William Wallace Cook, *Plotto: The Master Book of All Plots* (Portland, OR: Tin House Books, 2011), 1.
[2] Ibid., 4.

I scanned down. Cook, as Gordon had warned, had tried to summarize every plot he had ever heard of. And then some. For example:

(50) Being Impelled by an Unusual Motive to Engage In Crafty Enterprise
1

(a) (112) (117) (148.) (656)

A, poor, is in love with wealthy and aristocratic B * A, poor, in love with wealthy B, pretends to be a man of wealth (187) (228) (233) (347a-*)

(b) (171) (734) (1106 -*ch B to A) (1146)

A, of humble birth, falls in love with aristocratic B * A, of humble birth, in love with aristocratic B, pretends to be a man of high social standing ** (139) (153) (209) (1200)[3]

And so on, for three hundred pages of miniature print.

Plotto should have been called *Blotto*, because that was how I felt after trying to read it. "Gordon," I said, "this is not helpful. Aren't there some general rules of writing that a person can apply every time? Something *simple*?"

"Well," he said, "There is an old rule that says the second-act curtain is the darkest hour."

"What does that mean?"

"That's all I know. The end of the second act is the hero's darkest hour."

I pondered that. It sounded like there was something there, but I didn't know what.

I decided to use the notion as a wedge. If I could figure out what a "darkest hour" was, maybe I would learn something important about plot construction. So I thought very hard about everything I had ever heard about story structure, which was precious little. One favored technique was to divide the story

---

[3] Ibid., 24.

into three acts; I had heard that one on numerous occasions, and it was a method I used myself. I didn't know a logical reason for it, but intuitively, three acts seemed to produce more satisfying results than two acts or four or whatever. On the first couple of screenplays I wrote, it had never occurred to me to divide them into acts. But when I started partitioning them that way, the stories seemed to have more narrative drive. By the time I wrote *Alien*, I had used the three-act structure once or twice and liked the results. *Alien* was in three acts. The end of *Alien's* second act was the "chest-burster" scene, which was the most intense scene in the story. But was that the "darkest hour"? Well, things certainly got worse for the humans at that point. Then, eventually, they got better. I guessed that would qualify as a "darkest hour." But could I be sure?

Either way, I now had two rules: (1) three acts and (2) the "darkest hour" at the conclusion of the second act. Anything else?

Well, one thing I had gradually picked up from talking to movie professionals was the notion of "conflict." Conflict was necessary to keep your story from getting boring. It's boring watching people just have a good time. They should always be in trouble in a story, and this trouble was usually referred to as "conflict."

So… three acts. Darkest hour. Conflict. What did this all add up to?

I started pushing the pieces around.

If the second-act curtain was the "darkest hour," then what was the first-act curtain? And what was the *third*-act curtain, a.k.a. the end of the movie? And what, if anything, did the "darkest hour" have to do with conflict?

What *was* conflict?

"Analyze" means "to take apart." Like a physicist chopping an atom into quarks, I set out to dissect "conflict" into its smallest possible components.

First, I reasoned, you must have *characters*. Then you have to have something for them to come into *conflict* about. That is, "conflict" is when two people are at each other's throats over *something*, over *an issue*. They disagree about the best way to resolve the "issue": One guy thinks it should be handled one way, the other guy thinks a different solution is the way to go. That would be a *conflict*. In *Alien*, for example, the "issue" would be what to do with the humans. The humans think they should stay alive and unmolested; the alien has a different view. (Ash, the android, takes a complicated middle-ground view; he's not openly antagonistic toward the humans like the alien is, but he eventually decides, under orders from the corporation they all work for, that the humans are "expendable"). That would constitute the movie's conflict.

Conflict: When two characters or groups of characters disagree about how to resolve an "issue."

Now, what about this three-act business? How did conflict plug into that? Or, were three acts just a way to give you smaller pieces to work with? That didn't seem like a very powerful use of acts; if you have three acts, surely you ought to really *do* something with them.

Well… Gordon had said that the "darkest hour," whatever that was, came at the end of the second act. Not the first act, or the third: the *second*. And not the beginning of the act, or the middle: the *end* of the second act. "Curtain" was the word he used, just like in live theater when an actual physical curtain drops, leaving the audience buzzing about what's going to happen next — sort of a cliffhanger effect.

But what was a "darkest hour" redefined in terms of conflict? I guessed you could say that when the conflict reaches its most extreme point of crisis, your hero is experiencing the "darkest hour." So now I replaced the term "darkest hour" with "moment of greatest conflict."

Now I extrapolated backwards: What about the end of the *first* act? Surely something ought to happen there, too? What could I do with the conflict at the end of Act One? Maybe I could have the conflict gel at that point? Spend the first act laying out the various pieces of the conflict, and when the final piece clicks into place, that's the first-act curtain? But shouldn't I establish the conflict right at the beginning of the story? If absence of conflict was boring, didn't I need to have conflict from the very first frame? I could show somebody quarreling over something, and then spend the rest of Act One explaining how it came about.

However, by this point in my screenwriting career, I already had a recurrent problem with shooting off all my ammunition too early in the story, leaving me with nowhere to go in the second half of the script. I had tentatively concluded that it was better to sacrifice some excitement up front, to ration it out with a certain frugality, so that by the time I got to the last act, I could hit my audience hardest with the mostest. Better to kick off low and wrap up high than start with a bang and end with a whimper. It was a question of audience fatigue. It's tiring to watch a movie (especially an action movie), so to maintain the viewer's interest, you have to keep raising the ante. If I have spent the first two acts peaking the meter, nothing I write in the third act, no matter how frantic, can possibly be exciting enough to compensate for audience overstimulation and keep the blitzed-out viewer's attention from flagging.

So I figured, okay, let's say nothing special has to be going on when the movie starts. The audience is fresh and willing to give you some rope to hang yourself with. Why not take advantage of that initial tolerance? Spend the first act sketching in the characters and the situation, showing how an "issue of contention" arises, and how the characters come to cross-purposes over it? Suddenly, they'll be in "conflict," and the audience's interest will abruptly peak.

So we've defined the conflict, and now we're in Act Two. What happens next?

Well, somehow, the second act has to lead to a *"most extreme moment of conflict."* This event will heighten the tension and boost the audience's level of engagement. Then I can rocket for the end – which would obviously resolve the conflict!

I started to get excited. I had something here. If only I could figure out what it was.

The crux of it all was that "moment of greatest conflict." How could I differentiate that from the first-act curtain, when the conflict was *defined*? I didn't want to just repeat the first-act curtain by restating the conflict. That would be dull; they already know what the damn conflict is. What I wanted was to somehow transform the conflict into a new and more intense kind of conflict. *But how?*

It took me a while to pull that one out of the fog, but here's what I finally came up with: Suppose that after the conflict is first defined, the antagonists can still walk away from it if they want to. They hate each other's guts, but if push comes to shove, they can always say, "Ahh, screw it" and go home. The conflict only continues at this point because they're too pig-headed to quit, but they always have a way out if they really want to take it.

Now, let's suppose that, as a result of their going at each other hammer and tongs for two acts, the situation finally deteriorates to a point *where backing away from the conflict is no longer possible.* In short, all this squabbling makes everything come to a head, the situation takes a sudden turn for the worse, and now it's too late to walk away! They have to fight to the death! That would raise the conflict to a whole new level — they're *trapped!* — and it would be the perfect setup for a concluding battle to the finish!

Now I had it.

I changed my terminology one more time. No longer was it the "darkest hour" or the "moment of greatest conflict." It was now *The Point of No Return*.

NOW THIS WASN'T A "FORMULA," EXACTLY; it wasn't cut-and-dried enough to qualify as one. It was a *system*. And the thing to do with my new system was to try it out and see if it worked.

My first opportunity came not on a script of my own, but on a thing Ronnie Shusett was fooling around with called *Phobia*. He had bought this amateur effort from a tyro writer for a pittance, and he had managed to get a Canadian production company interested in buying it… if he could fix it. He brought it over for me to read and said he would throw a few bucks my way if I could help make it work.

I looked it over and found a creaking jumble of Z-movie clichés. Raising it to the level of even a B-movie would be an immense chore. But if my new theory was right, such a total overhaul might not be necessary. If I could make the script fit my new three-act system, maybe it would work on its own terms. So I gave Ronnie a rundown of my system, and we talked over the extent to which *Phobia* met the criteria I had devised.

First, we identified the conflict. (A crazy psychologist is trying to kill one of his patients.) Then we divided the script into three acts, like cutting a sausage in three pieces with a knife, and we found that the script failed to address its conflict anywhere near the first- and second-act curtains. It did address things at the end; the hero defeats the villain. But at the one-third and two-thirds marks, the script was concerned with just about everything *except* the conflict. So I said, "What's the easiest thing we can do to draw the conflict back on board at those two points?"

We rooted around in the script and found the scene where the conflict first matured — the moment where we, the audience, first became aware that this story was about Guy A versus Guy B — and we moved that scene to the end of the first act, about a third of the way into the script. Then I went to the end of the second act (the two-thirds mark, more or less) and made up a brand new scene where the good guy and bad guy suddenly get frozen into a showdown. I banged it out on my old tank-like IBM Model B and handed it to Ronnie. "Stick it right in there," I said, marking the page. Ronnie went off and had the script retyped with my changes.

He came back over, waving the script like a flag. "It works!" he shrieked. "It works!" So I read it. And I found that a strange and amazing thing had happened: The quality of the writing in the script hadn't changed at all. It was the same lousy script, in the same words, except in the couple of places we had intervened. But somehow... the script had become *interesting*. "Hey!" I said. "This is pretty good!" The real excitement for me, of course, was in seeing my system validated. Apparently it had the power to transform a sow's ear I didn't want to watch... into a sow's ear I *did* want to watch. Like a gambler who wins on his first pull at the slot machine, I was hooked on my own system, and I have used it ever since.

(The postscript to *Phobia*, by the way, is this: When Ron submitted the new script to the Canadian producer, he promptly bought it and hired John Huston to direct; however, at that point, the producer decided that he himself was a screenwriter of no mean ability [How hard could screenwriting be, after all, if *screenwriters* could do it?], and so he sat down and completely rewrote the script, based not on any system but only on his own magnificent intuitions. Ron read it and found it was now even worse than before we worked on it, so he called up Huston and suggested he read our draft because it was better. Huston, whose stated attitude in such situations was "take the money and run," said, "I don't care, and it's too much trouble to argue with this guy." So he went ahead and directed the producer's script. And it was a ripe stinker of a tomcat's B.M., and it lost every dime. But it was the *producer's* every dime. He wanted it; he got it. Some producers are like that. They walk around with a knife strapped to their own throats, and every time their vanity twitches a little, they give the knife an exploratory shove.)

Now, I have written good scripts and bad scripts. I have even written mediocre scripts. In her book *You'll Never Eat Lunch in This Town Again*, Julia Phillips says that *Edgar*, which I wrote for her, was "a piece of shit... some of the worst work in his life."[4] She was talking through her hat, because she never read the worst thing I ever wrote. If she had, I guarantee she would have looked more kindly upon poor *Edgar*. There was a period of time in the '80s when I was going from one studio assignment to the next, writing whatever the brass would pay me for. More than once, I thought a script I had written on assignment was a washout, that my system had failed to rescue it from narrative collapse. Given my attitude toward those scripts, you won't be surprised to learn that I threw them in the corner and never looked at them again. Recently, though, while cleaning out my office, I unearthed several of the things and, out of curiosity, reread them. Enough years had passed since I wrote these scripts that I had a nice fresh perspective. And, to my surprise and pleasure — and you'll have to take my word for this — *every single one of those scripts worked*. If they'd been filmed, you could sit right through to the end and have a fine time. In most cases, there was some actual solid reason why they couldn't be produced, but it wasn't because they didn't work.

One example of a script you wouldn't want to film now is *Atlantis*, written by Don Jakoby and me for Fox in 1986. *Atlantis* was about a high-tech Navy mission to the deepest part of the ocean, where a civilization based on exotic technology is discovered. In other words, it's a story just like *The Abyss*, which was filmed shortly after we finished writing *Atlantis*. Sad to say, the world doesn't need another *Abyss*, and besides, history got away from this one. The script's whole premise, the central metaphor from which everything unfolded, was Cold War rivalry between the United States and the U.S.S.R. (the aforementioned Navy mission's goal is to snatch a state-of-the-art Soviet sub that has

---

[4]Julia Phillips, *You'll Never Eat Lunch In This Town Again* (New York: Random House, 1991), 496.

come to grief); the personal problems of the characters, as well as the difficulties faced by the "Atlans," as we called them, were all iterations of U.S.-Soviet antagonisms. If you tried to disentangle these Cold War elements, you wouldn't have much of a script left. Just in case any of my Gentle Readers missed it, there is no more Soviet Union, no more Cold War, and nothing obvious to take their places in dramatic fiction. So, at present, this is not a script you would really be able to film. But it's a good script! Really, it works. This scene of group telepathy, for example, is downright uncanny:

INT. A ROOM IN ATLEA - DAY

Eloa (an Atlan woman) leads Nick Cooper (marine biologist, 30s) and Viktor (Russian pilot) into a small white chamber.

                    NICK
          What is it?

                    ELOA
          You may find this illuminating.

In the center of the chamber is a low table. On the table rests a pyramid-shaped crystal.

                    ELOA
          The crystal was an intermediate step
          for us on the way to full consciousness.
          Over a limited region it allows any set
          of beings, no matter how low on the
          evolutionary scale, to read thought.
          We no longer need them.

Lieutenant Kress (Naval Intelligence) is led in by Chamuel (Atlan man).

                          CHAMUEL
              Come. Sit.

They all sit around the table. The five of
them. The crystal in the center of the table.
Bluish, faceted. A suggestion of inner fire.

Kress looks at it warily.

                           NICK
              What's the range on it?

                           ELOA
              Approximately fifteen feet.

                          KRESS
                     (suspicious)
              And what's it do?

                           NICK
              It reads minds, Kress.

Kress scoffs.

                           NICK
                     (to Eloa)
              What do we do now?

                           ELOA
              Just sit quietly.

Five people looking at each other – sitting
in a circle.

                    KRESS
               (stares at object)
        Hey, what are we doing…?

                    CHAMUEL
         Try and guess what the other
         person is thinking.

Looks all around.

They focus their attention on the crystal.
Gaze into it.

Gazing INTO THE CRYSTAL – it appears to have
infinite depths. Shimmering patterns – like
the forms in a human mind – going on forever.
A window into a crystal universe. Alive.

Suddenly it happens: THE FIRST THOUGHT –
ZINGS! through space and is HEARD in each of
their heads. No lips moving – just thoughts
popping into space – heard –

As the pace accelerates – two – then three
– then four overlapping cross thoughts –

Their startled expressions as thoughts grow
on thoughts – opening them up –

        K   N
What a crock   Incredible

            K
        What?

                                        N
                              I can read Kress's

          K
Oh shit!
Who's that?

                        V
                You can hear
                him thinking

          N
It works

                        N
                Wow... Hi, Kress

                                                K
                                        Kill ugly
                                                No

                                K
                        Piss

          N
    Eloa

                                                K
                                        Oh no

          K
I hate you cooper

                  E
        Hello cooper

         K
      Control

 K
Sex

     V
   Amazing! Is it not?

            K
        Loss of control

  N   K
I love you   This is an order

K   K
Steal   They'll know

  E
I love you too

  N   V
You do?   Know what?

           K
       They'll all know

  E
Yes.

 K
No!

    N
Take it easy

```
                K
Wow uh Russians Mom cheese air
stop it stop no have to stop this   N
oh man stop fuck can't stop         Uh oh
goddamn I'm going crazy get out
of my mind I'm going to steal it
NO I CAN'T STAND IT
V
What's he
going to steal?


                KRESS
            (screams)
      YOU ALL KNOW WHAT I'M THINKING!

Kress jumps up and bolts from the room,
knocking over his chair.

                ELOA
            Enough.

Eloa steps forward and puts her hand over
the crystal. Immediately the thought-symphony
stops.
```

I remember how much trouble we were having with the second half of *Atlantis*, how heavily I relied on my system to guide us through to The End, and how uncertain I was that it helped. Well... it helped.

So I am going to lay out my story-structural system in complete schematic detail — and you can judge it for yourself. If you don't like it — if you think there is nothing fundamental or universal about my system — that it's just a personal quirk of mine, then you have nothing to lose by ignoring it. Use another structure. Write your story in four and a half acts. Don't use any acts at all. Abandon your conflict halfway through your script and switch to a completely different conflict, which you don't resolve; or, ignore the whole notion of conflict altogether. See how much skin it takes off my nose.

And *Plotto*? It's the kind of idea that always appeals to a certain mind-set, and the arrival of computers made its re-birth inevitable, as digital processing obviously lends itself to such applications. *Plotto's* modern-day avatars are called "idea generators." Two software packages inspired by the same phi-losophy that galvanized Cook are Storybase (formerly known as Plots Unlimited) and Dramatica. Storybase is a situational generation program allowing you to enter characters, actions, and "mind-sets" into a pull-down menu system that then sug-gests situations that such conditions would create within your story. According to www.storybase.net, this system has the ca-pability of generating over 3,900 potential narrative situations based on data the writer inputs. Dramatica works by a process of elimination, on the principle that the writer must sort through all possible stories before settling on the best one; the software is essentially a "story engine" that asks the writer questions and presents story options based on the answers provided. When all options are exhausted, Dramatica maps out a rough draft of your screenplay-to-be.

These programs, like the rest of the screenwriting packages on the market, boast heavy-hitting endorsements. Storybase is hailed as "a smart program" by script consultant Christopher Vogler and is praised by *Scr(i)pt* and *EMMY* Magazines. Dra-matica received an "Excellent" rating from *Writer's Digest*, and *Back Stage West* said it "may teach you more about the intrica-cies of the writing craft than any other product on the market." In an article for *U.S News and World Report*, Amy Saltzman and Edward Baig praised the philosophy of idea-generation software, speculating on what Shakespeare, Edison, or Picasso

might have accomplished with such technology at their fingertips.[5] My suspicion is that it would have stopped them dead
in their tracks. I mean, if a machine can replicate the creative
process, why bother? Just turn the thing on and go to the pub.
When choices are required, your pet monkey can randomly
punch the keys. Bearing in mind that everybody in the world
potentially has access to the same machines, the philosophy
here seems to be that whoever pushes the button first gets to be
Picasso.

But the manufacturers claim these programs don't write
your story for you. Really? Sounds to me like you throw a dart at
the machine, it spits out some choices, you throw another dart,
and so on. Then the machine extrudes a scene-by-scene story
outline, and you just fill in character names and write dialogue.
These things are part of the ongoing, transvocational effort to
replace humans with machines. Do they work? Beats me. But if
I had to crank out lots of scripts under pressure for, say, a TV
series, I would probably try them out. Wouldn't you?

---

[5] Amy Saltzman and Edward Baig, "Plugging In To 'Creativity,'" *US News and World
Report*, October 29, 1990.

EXERCISES: LOOKING FOR THE FORMULA

1. Examine the structure of your favorite film and note the endpoints of the three acts. What occurs at the end of the first act that defines the conflict of the story?

_____

_____

_____

What is the moment at the end of the second act, at which the characters can no longer back away from the conflict (a.k.a. The Point of No Return)?

_____

_____

_____

What occurs at the end of the film's third act that resolves the conflict?

_____

_____

_____

2. Give a brief summary of this film's conflict. What is the issue among the characters, and what are their differing opinions on how that issue should be addressed?

_____

_____

_____

3. Can you name a bad movie with a script that "works"? (Conflict markers are in the right spots, film has an appropriate Point of No Return)...

_____

_____

_____

Chapter Two

TOWARD A DEFINITION OF STRUCTURE,
or Let's NOT Get Physical

Screenwriting is carpentry.

— William Goldman

UNTIL I STARTED WRITING THIS BOOK, it never occurred to me that I might have to define the word "structure." It seems kind of self-explanatory. But nevertheless, here goes . . .

Story structure is a set of predefined relationships between story elements that give shape to the finished story.

As an architectural term, "structure" refers to the beams and walls that hold a building together. The structure of a house performs two functions: (1) it defines the shape of the house, and (2) it holds the pieces of the house together. The analogy to story structure is an exact one; however, the structure of a house is a manifest physical object that you can see with the naked eye. If you knock a hole in the wall, you can see the beams and cross-braces that make up the house's structure. Some parts of the structure of a house are not even hidden; certain beams and supports are exposed. In the graphic arts, structure usually takes the form of an under-sketch. There are, of course, all kinds of art, but in many traditional forms, such as Italian Renaissance painting, the under-sketch is hidden. The artist starts out with a pencil drawing on the canvas; that is the picture's structure, although artists don't use that terminology (they speak instead of "composition"). By the time the artist gets through putting down the paint, the under-sketch is no longer readily visible. But it's not absolutely unseeable; you could view it by X-raying the canvas, the way art conservators do.

But in a story, an X-ray would reveal nothing because the structure is not physical. It is conceptual — an abstraction. Story structure is made of words, but those words are not in the script. They are floating in the writer's head, or spoken by collaborators or studio executives, or written in a story outline or treatment. The only way to detect a story's structure is for a knowledgeable person to examine the story and infer that structure from the story's visible parts, those little marks of ink that describe places and characters and dialogue and events.

(Even so, a piece of a story's structure is occasionally visible. In a book, "Chapter One" at the top of a page is a visible piece of structure. Rarely is this signal offered in the movies, but if you wanted to — actually, if the producer wanted to — you could stick captions up on the screen that said "Act One," "Act Two," and so on. If you did, these would be visible fragments of story structure. Woody Allen used on-screen captions in *Hannah and Her Sisters* to create separate sections of the film, as did Quentin Tarantino in *Pulp Fiction*. The captions that are on virtually every film released — the film's title, the names of the people who worked on it, and so forth — are not structure. They're just labels, letting the audience know that a film was, say, "written by Dan O'Bannon," just like the label on a can tells you that it contains "Campbell's Pork & Beans," or what have you.)

If you omit the structure from a house, it will collapse. It won't even stand up in the first place. So nobody ever leaves out the structure when building a house. But if you leave out the structure when writing a screenplay, nothing that obvious will happen. Superficially, it looks the same as a structured script; the pages won't go flying apart or anything. Not until later, when you start inflicting that screenplay on other people, will you realize your story has collapsed.

*Story structure is an **invisible** construct that describes the relationships between parts of the story.* It is a dressmaking pattern that shows you where your story's arms and legs go, a stencil that points out the locations of the little (or big) windows inside which you can be creative. It was invented in order to get the audience to sit through a movie all the way to the end.

More elegantly, story structure is a way to make certain your story's themes are realized and fulfilled. If something is missing, structure will show you exactly what's missing and where. It is formal and restricting, yes, but empowering as well. And that's what this book is about: the power of story structure. Or, really, the power it gives *you*.

EXERCISE: TOWARD A DEFINITION OF STRUCTURE
Name a film that uses on-screen structural markers (chapter headings, metacinematic scene changes, etc.). How do these markers function in defining the structure of the film? Do they operate like conventional act-break markers, or do they create their own unique structural system?

_____

_____

_____

_____

_____

_____

_____

_____

_____

_____

_____

Chapter Three

OTHER PEOPLE'S SYSTEMS,
or For Those Who Bought My Book by Mistake

*If you leave the smallest corner of your head vacant for a moment,
other people's opinions will rush in from all quarters.*

— George Bernard Shaw

GRANTED, MY SYSTEM IS NOT THE WORLD ENTIRE, so before I lay it out for you, let's see what some other people have to say about story structure. There are six authorities whose names come up most frequently in discussions of dramatic structure. Five of them have written their own books on the subject. (The sixth is Ibsen, whom we'll discuss in Chapter Seven.) Let's take a look at these five now. They all have useful things to say about making stories work.

ARISTOTLE: The Plot's the Thing

*Any realistic notion of tragic drama must start from the fact
of catastrophe. Tragedies end badly. The tragic personage
is broken... Tragedy is irreparable. It cannot lead to just
and material compensation for past suffering.*

— George Steiner, *The Death of Tragedy*

ARISTOTLE'S *POETICS*, WRITTEN 2,300 YEARS AGO IN GREEK, is the earliest study we have of the craft of drama.[6] Our ideas have evolved since then. Plus, in its raw form, the *Poetics*

---

[6] My quotations are mostly taken (with a bit of paraphrasing) from the translation of the *Poetics* by Preston H. Epps (Chapel Hill: University of North Carolina Press, 1942, 1970).

is pretty confusing. Aristotle is sometimes rambling here; these seem to be class lecture notes. But the big A has some solid ideas and is worth a discussion, if only out of curiosity. (Because the *Poetics* is in public domain, I will be quoting rather extensively from the text itself. Why buy a cow, right?)

Aristotle believes that the origin of drama lies in people's natural predilection for the art of "mimicry," by which he means any type of representative portrayal — from portrait painting to dancing to birdcalls. The particular art form called *drama* is explained as a "mimicry of human actions." He says that tragedy evolved from epic poetry (like the *Iliad* and the *Odyssey*), and that Sophocles introduced painted scenery to the stage.

Action

Tragedy, Aristotle informs us, is a "mimicry of actions of noble characters" which, through the generation of pity and terror, brings about a "catharsis" or purgation of the emotions on the part of the audience. This intense outpouring is designed to leave the viewer drained and limp, which is the "special kind of pleasure" afforded by tragedy.[7]

Tragedy, then, portrays *action* that springs from two causes: *character* and *thought*. "It is because of these," says Aristotle, "that all men fail or succeed." He defines character as "habitual action," whereas "thought" is "everything the characters say." You can see Aristotle struggling to clarify his thinking here — but hey, nobody had ever written anything like this before. Drama hadn't even been around for very long, and this attempt was the earliest anybody had tried to make sense of it.

The Six Parts of Tragedy

Aristotelian tragedy is comprised of six elements:

(1) Plot ("by 'plot' I mean the arrangement of the incidents");

(2) Character indicators ("that by which we determine what kinds of men are being presented");

---

[7] Francis Fergusson, in his introductory essay to Samuel Henry Butcher's translation of the *Poetics* (New York: Macmillan, 1961), 7.

(3) Thought ("everything the characters say when they present an argument or make evident an opinion");

(4) Spectacle, meaning stage effects like blood;

(5 and 6) Diction and song, which are irrelevant to our present discussion.

None of this information is much help to the screenwriter.

Plot

"But the most important of these," according to Aristotle, "is the arrangement of the incidents of the *plot*, for tragedy is not the portrayal of men as such, but of action, of life." He continues:

> Happiness and misery are the result of *action*... Men are the kinds of individuals they are as a result of their character; but they become happy or miserable as a result of their *actions*. Consequently [since the purpose of tragedy is to show how men become happy or unhappy, and since it is their *actions* which bring this about], dramatists do not employ action in order to achieve character portrayal, but they include character because of its relation to action.

(Aristotle had obviously never been to story meetings with studio executives pounding the drum: "Character! Character! Character!") "Therefore, the incidents and plot constitute the end of tragedy... without action there could be no tragedy, but there *could* be tragedy without character." (Whatever that means!) "In other words: if anyone should arrange, in proper order, a number of speeches which showed moral character... *he would not achieve the end of tragedy*. This end would be much better achieved by a tragedy which was deficient in these elements, yet had a plot and arrangement of incidents... Therefore, the first principle and, as it were, the soul of tragedy is the *plot*." The reasoning is extremely garbled here, but all he's saying is: less gab, more action. And, as any screenwriter who's been endlessly advised to "show, don't tell" knows all too well, he's right.

Character Indicators

A character indicator is any action that illustrates a person's *choice*. As our Greek philosopher says, "Therefore, speeches in which a character is in no way confronted with something he must choose or reject, do not have character indicators."

The tragic character must be "good," as proven by some choice he has made. "This quality of good is possible in every class of persons; for even a slave or a woman may be good."[8]

The Three Unities

Aristotle says that tragedy imitates an action that is "whole and complete."

"A whole is that which has a beginning, a middle and an end" — three acts, in other words, although he never refers to them as such. At least he has a reason for this structure that he can put into words. The best I can say is that I do it because it feels right. (See Chapter Eleven for more on this subject.)

Next, Aristotle expounds on *the three unities* of a dramatic work: unity of *place*, *time*, and *action*. Simply put, the play is set in a single locale, on a single day, and features nothing inessential to the plot. The nature of cinematic storytelling has altered the function of these unities quite a bit, but for completeness's sake, we will review them here.

Unity of Place

The Greeks weren't too adept at scene changes, so their plays only had one set, usually the front of a temple. Thanks to modern film editing (not to mention advances in transportation since Aristotle's day), a single dramatic story can now take place all over the world. Some stories would in fact be virtually straitjacketed by confinement to a single location. Can you imagine a James Bond picture in which 007 never leaves M's office?

Unity of Time

Tragedy, Aristotle says, "tries as far as possible to limit the time of its action to one revolution of the sun or to depart only

---

[8] In this quotation, I have blended Epps's translation with that of Butcher (New York: Hill & Wang, 1961), 81.

slightly from that rule." In other words, a story's action shouldn't unfold over more than a day of dramatic time. This is a rule of storytelling that, once again, has been greatly altered by the cinematic medium. Film stories can now take place over the span of years, decades, even millennia. In one of the most famous moments in film history, the narrative of Stanley Kubrick's *2001* encompasses millions of years in the space of a single edit. Still, you can achieve a great deal of intensity and focus — ferocity even — by keeping your time frame short. One of my own scripts, the yet-to-be-produced *Omnivore*, takes place in fewer than 24 hours, from just before sunset until after dawn the next day. It gives the impression of playing out in real time, which some films, in fact, do (We'll discuss one of these, *The Set-Up*, in detail in Chapter Eleven.)

Unity of Action

"Furthermore... the different parts of the action must be so related to each other that if any part is changed or taken away the whole will be altered and disturbed. For anything whose presence or absence makes no discernible difference is no essential part of the whole." Now, this rule still more or less holds in modern storytelling; it's remained a pretty unshakable cornerstone of screenwriting for decades. Don't believe me? Try putting a completely superfluous musical number into your gritty action-thriller screenplay. Then see what the story department tells you to cut first.

Probability and Necessity

"Of simple plots and actions, the episodic are the worst. By an 'episodic' plot, I mean one in which the episodes are not arranged according to the law of probability and necessity. Poor poets make such plots because of their poor ability...."

Good poets (Aristotle's term for storytellers), however, construct their plots with episodes that "are brought about one by the other. For anything so brought about will appear more wonderful than if it happens spontaneously or by chance, since, of the things which happen by chance, those seem to excite more wonder which appear to have happened in accordance with some design, such as when the statue of Mitys in Argos fell on the murderer of Mitys and killed him... Therefore, this type of plot must necessarily be the best." So Aristotle, in a slightly linguistically gummy way, is an advocate for cause-and-effect plotting. (It is interesting to note that Aristotle's criterion of dramatic worth is "excitement of wonder"— a.k.a. audience response).

Fear & Pity: The Tragic Character

Now for his famous dictum about *pity* and *fear*:

> But tragedies are imitations [i.e. depictions] not only of actions which are complete, but of such as inspire pity and fear, and actions inspire the most pity and fear whenever they [1] happen contrary to expectation and [2] are brought about one by the other.... Since the plot of the best type of tragedy... must be a depiction of actions which arouse pity and fear – this being the distinctive mark of tragic mimicry – it is evident, first of all that [1] *flawlessly good men* must not be shown passing from good into evil fortune, for that arouses neither pity nor fear, but merely shock and aversion. Nor [2] must evil men be shown passing from adversity into good fortune [for this will inspire only moral outrage]. Nor again [3] should the downfall of the *utter villain* be exhibited; a plot of this kind would, doubtless, satisfy the moral sense, but it would inspire neither pity nor fear; for pity is aroused by the plight of the man who *does not entirely deserve his misfortune*, and fear by the predicaments of men like ourselves... The only type of situation left is that midway between these just mentioned: it is the situation of the man of glory and good fortune, who [on the one hand] is not unadulteratedly superior in excellence and uprightness, yet who [on the other hand] does not come into his misfortune because of viciousness or depravity, but through some error or frailty.[9]

---

[9] In the preceding quotation, I have commingled Epps with Butcher (p. 75–76) and a little paraphrasing.

Or, as Howard and Mabley (more on them shortly) put it with the succinctness of two extra millennia, the ideal tragic protagonist is "a character who is less than perfect but somewhat short of utterly despicable."[10]

Change of Fortune

Tragedy, then, depicts the downfall of a character, his passage from good fortune into adversity. This genre places a *change of fortune* at the center of tragic action. Today, we might call this a *twist*. The dramatist may employ two types of action to bring about this change: *reversals* and *recognitions*. As Aristotle explains it:

> A *reversal* is a change… by which the action veers around in the opposite direction, and that in accordance with the laws of probability or necessity, just as, in *Oedipus Rex*, the servant who comes to cheer the king and free him of his fear of his mother by telling him who he is, accomplishes just the opposite…. As the name suggests, a *recognition* is a change by which those slated by the plot for good or bad fortune pass from a state of ignorance into a state of knowledge which disposes them either to friendship or enmity towards each other. The best type of recognition is one which is accompanied by reversal, such as happens in *Oedipus Rex*. There are, of course, recognitions of other things also… but the recognition especially related to plot and action is the one defined above; for such recognitions will arouse either pity or fear. For tragedy is a depiction of just such actions as arouse pity and fear, and it is the same sort of action which will bring about good and bad fortune…. Now if the action is one of an enemy against an enemy, there is nothing, either in the act or in its intention, to arouse pity, unless it be the mere suffering. The same would be true in the case of those who were neither friends nor foes.

Tough guy, that Aristotle.

---

[10] Howard and Mabley, *The Tools of Screenwriting: A Writer's Guide to the Craft and Elements of a Screenplay* (New York: St. Martin's Griffin, 1993).

Aristotle continues:

> But whenever the tragic action is against a member of the
> family, such as when a brother either kills or intends to kill
> a brother, a son a father, a mother a son or a son a mother,
> or some other deed of this kind, these are the materials
> for which the tragic poet must be on the lookout.... One
> arrangement is to have the deed done, as it was in early
> tragedies, by characters who are entirely conscious and
> aware of what they are doing, as Euripides has Medea kill
> her children, fully aware of what she is doing. A second
> arrangement is to have the characters do the terrible deed
> but do it in ignorance and later discover their relation-
> ship... The third choice is to have the character on the
> verge of doing some irreparable deed through ignorance
> and then discover what he is about to do before he does
> it... The poorest arrangement artistically is to have a char-
> acter knowingly intend to do something and then not do
> it. It is abhorrent but not tragic, since no tragic deed hap-
> pens... The next best choice is to have the character do the
> deed. It is better for him to do it in ignorance and discover
> the true situation later; for the recognition is startling. The
> third and last choice is the best. I mean such as that of
> Merope in *Cresphontes*, who is about to kill her son but
> discovers who he is before she kills him.... The two parts
> of a plot which are concerned with these matters are, then,
> reversals and recognitions. But there is a third element...

The Tragic Experience

"The tragic experience is: *destructive or painful actions such
as deaths in plain view, extreme pain, wounds and the like.*"
This definition is consistent with the findings of psychologist
James Gilligan, author of a well-regarded series of books on
the phenomenon and psychology of violence, who declares
that "tragic drama is always violent."[11] So, by this definition,

---

[11] James Gilligan, M.D., *Violence: Reflections on a National Epidemic* (New York:
Vintage Books, 1997), 6.

The Texas Chain Saw Massacre is one of the most tragic of all stories; it has extreme violence, deaths in plain view, reversals and recognitions... but no noble characters. (Sorry, Tobe.)

Denouement

Aristotle continues: "These reversals and recognitions must grow out of the arrangement of the plot itself, by its being so constructed that each succeeding incident happens necessarily or according to probability from what has happened previously; for it makes a great deal of difference whether the incidents happen *because* of what has preceded or merely *after* it.... It is evident, therefore, that the denouement [resolution] of a plot must result naturally from the plot itself and not from a *deus ex machina*, as in *Medea*, nor as it happens in the return in the *Iliad*." In ancient Greek drama, a *deus ex machina* (literally "god from machine") was a crane that swung down onto the stage carrying an actor, decked out as a divinity, who solved all the characters' problems by fiat. Today this well-known term refers to anything that intrudes from outside the events of the story to resolve it at the last moment. This device is still frowned upon because it often leaves the viewers feeling cheated; it has invested its emotions and its best thinking into the characters' quandaries, only to have all that work turn out irrelevant to the outcome. (But I do feel obligated to mention that a lifetime of watching and making movies has taught me that, under the right circumstances, a *deus ex machina* works fine. Here comes the cavalry, and so forth.)

"Every tragedy," says Aristotle, "has [1] complication and [2] denouement... By 'complication' I mean everything from the beginning of the play up to the last part of the action just before the change of fortune. The denouement consists of everything from the beginning of the change of fortune to the end of the play." *Denouement* is a French word (translating some Greek word of Aristotle) meaning "untying (as with a knot)" and refers to the outcome of the story. Within my three-act structure, the denouement probably wouldn't start until The

Point of No Return — that is, it would constitute the third act. I have also heard the term used as a synonym for "epilogue," that is, a brief scene at the very end, after the story's conflict is resolved, that allows the audience members to unwind before climbing out of their seats and heading home. Because its meaning is fuzzy, I generally try to stay away from the word "denouement."

AT THIS POINT, ARISTOTLE'S DISCUSSION pretty much dribbles out. And that's the *Poetics*. When all is said and done, it's an arcane work, certainly of historical interest, but for screenwriting purposes, much of it is either loony or so long ago digested into our dramaturgy that we don't even have to think about it consciously any more.

That said, Aristotle's emphasis on action is very cinematic, and I do like his specificity. These are rules you can really work with. His prescription for characterization, for instance, is this: *"Character indicators are those ACTIONS which demonstrate a person's CHOICES – what things he chooses or rejects, for good or for evil."* Compare Howard and Mabley: "The essence of characterization is the revelation of the inner life of the character." Well, great, but they don't tell you how to make that revelation happen. Aristotle does: You make your character *choose*.

EXERCISE: ARISTOTLE

Select a favorite film and analyze how its structure makes use of Aristotle's three unities. Does the film express a "unity of place" (being set in a particular building, a specific neighborhood, a single city, etc.)? Does the duration of the narrative, as expressed cinematically, convey a "unity of time?" Does the film obey the principle of "unity of action" by having no scenes or characters that are inessential to the plot?

LAJOS EGRI: Defeating the Thud

> *To catch a character in trouble and to tell about it*
> *is the basis for almost any story.*
>
> — Jesse Hill Ford

LAJOS EGRI ORIGINALLY PUBLISHED *The Art of Dramatic Writing* in 1942, which to some might make the book seem as old as Aristotle's *Poetics*. But Egri's book is as influential today as when he wrote it, and it makes its way onto lots of lists of essential "writing on writing."

Unlike some writers of how-to screenwriting books who have few if any produced credits to their names, Egri put some numbers on the scoreboard. He wrote his first three-act play at the age of ten, and wrote and directed stage works in both Europe and the United States for over thirty-five years. He also worked as a consultant for Hollywood screenwriters and served as director of the Egri School of Writing in New York City. *The Art of Dramatic Writing* (New York: Touchstone Books, 2004) is designed mainly for the playwright creating works for the stage, but many of its theories and ideas apply to screenwriting as well.

Character is Everything

Unlike Aristotle, who teaches that plot is the driving force behind all drama and that characters exist only to act out that plot, Egri believes (in common with virtually every other modern storytelling scholar) that character is the cornerstone of drama, so much so that the subtitle of his book describes dramatic writing's "Basis in the Creative Interpretation of Human Motives." To Egri, character is "the most interesting phenomenon anywhere," and any writer who tries to build characters around plots rather than the other way around will wind up with forced, melodramatic characters who do not live and breathe as authentic representations of the human condition.

Premise

Curiously, however, despite the primacy he gives to character, Egri does not believe that a play ultimately begins with its characters. Before anything else is decided about the play (characters, plot, setting, atmospherics), Egri asserts, the writer should develop a *premise* that he intends to prove through his drama. This premise is a simple idea, one that expresses a universal belief held by the author. ("Great love defies even death" is offered as a premise for *Romeo and Juliet*; Ibsen's *Ghosts* attempted to prove that "the sins of the father are visited on the children.") The writer must believe in his premise as an absolute truth, or his play will come across as false and contrived. According to Egri, once the premise is established, all of the other elements of the play should fall into place. The writer will know what kind of characters and plot are necessary to support the premise, and will be able to develop the natural progress of the drama to prove this premise. The premise thus serves as a kind of thumbnail thematic synopsis of the entire play.*

Hmm... that sounds like a *premise-driven* story system, not a *character-driven* one. In the wrong hands, this idea in action could result in preachy, stilted dramas with characters that do nothing but spout the playwright's opinions. Sensing this potential problem, Egri frequently retracts his statements about the primacy of the premise. After declaring how central the premise is to forming the resulting play, he says that the playwright doesn't have to start with a premise after all — he may construct his play around "a character or an incident, or even a simple thought." Then, he reverses himself all over again, stating that "it's impossible to know your characters" without a strong premise, and that once you choose a premise, "you and your characters become its slave." There's some sloppy thinking going on here. This idea is not fully digested, and Egri's uncertainty about character versus premise as the basis for his system could get the unwary writer into some trouble. One would be well advised to tread softly in implementing these theories about dramatic premise. (I personally believe that the

---

Alien's premise, Egri style, would be "Fools rush in where angels fear to tread."

premise, as defined by Egri, may be inherent to a good story but should not come first; you're probably better off letting the material find itself, and teasing the "premise" out of your characters and situation rather than vice versa.)

Back to Character

Despite fudging the issue of the character's supremacy as the linchpin of the drama, Egri makes it more than clear that character is, indeed, crucial to effective dramatic storytelling. He feels that character is shaped equally by *physical*, *social*, and *psychological* factors and that the writer must have a firm grasp on these three facets of his character's personality in order to render said character in three dimensions. Even if the playwright does not overtly include certain details, knowing them will be beneficial, as they may help to answer any pesky behavioral questions that may arise in constructing the story ("Would my character really do that?") He also believes that for characters to truly live and breathe, they must undergo *change*, that only in "the realm of bad writing" do characters "defy natural laws" and remain unaltered by the events that befall them. *Conflict* motivates this change; the decisions a character makes when faced with a challenge tell the audience who he is (which is just what Aristotle says as well: Choices act as what he calls "character indicators"). A character must also possess a strong enough will to see a conflict through to its resolution. Egri maintains that "the truly weak character is the person who will not fight because the pressure is not strong enough," and unless you put your character in circumstances that force him to see the conflict through, he will not be an effective engine for your drama. (That forced aspect — where the character has no choice but to resolve the conflict — is the essence of the Point of No Return concept.)

The Pivotal Character

For Egri, a play's *pivotal character* is whoever forces the conflict, who "takes the lead" in the fight, who wants something so badly "that he will destroy or be destroyed in the effort to attain his goal." This idea renders fascinatingly ambiguous the commonly held perception that "protagonist" and "antagonist" are synonymous with "hero" and "villain." Few would deny that Iago is the villain of *Othello*, but because he forces the conflict, he becomes Egri's "pivotal character," his "protagonist," whereas Othello becomes the "antagonist." Whether heroic or villainous, the pivotal character "is forced to be a pivotal character out of sheer necessity, and not because he wills it." His desire must be so great, and his proximity to his goal so far away, that only by forcing conflict can he possibly hope to reach this goal. Because the pivotal character begins the story already gunning for his goal, he necessarily evolves less than the other characters, because by virtue of knowing his goal, he is already close to the ultimate extreme when the story opens. Think of how little Iago changes over the course of Shakespeare's play, in contrast to Othello's wild rollercoaster ride.

Unity of Opposites

Egri states that in order for drama to be effective, characters must be properly "orchestrated" against one another. If you make your characters too similar in ideology, speech, or personal expression, the natural conflicts among them will be lessened and your dramatic effects diminished. But by properly pitting your characters against one another, the writer can achieve what Egri calls a "unity of opposites," in which the stalemate between protagonist and antagonist "can be broken only if one of the adversaries or both are exhausted, beaten or annihilated completely at the end." For a drama to achieve its fullest impact, the possibility of compromise between the opposing sides must be removed from the equation — either there is one victor, or both sides lose everything. If everyone wins, the fizz will go out of your story like stale champagne.

Point of Attack

Egri believes that it is crucial to begin your play at the proper "point of attack." A number of screenwriting gurus use this term with several different meanings. To Egri, "point of attack" means the start of your story, which should come at "the turning point in the life of one or more of your characters." If you waste time with static characters or enter your drama after the turning point has already passed... thud. Drama is like *Annie Hall's* relationship shark: It must be constantly on the move, or it dies.

Conflict

Of course, the basis of drama, and the jumping-off area for your point of attack, is *conflict*. Egri does not define conflict itself, but he does outline *four types* of conflict, only two of which are usable for the creation of dramatic works.

Slowly rising conflicts build tension to a breaking point at the climax, keeping the audience riveted to see how the action will escalate as the story progresses. (This description is actually a pretty good approximation of my own approach to creating dramatic conflict.) Also useful are *"foreshadowing" conflicts*, in which tensions between characters or knowledge of past events indicates a *potential conflict* that comes to a head as the story moves toward its climax. Writers should, however, avoid *static conflicts*, where the characters have no desires or do not know what they want, or *jumping conflicts*, where you leap so far ahead in your story that the passage from event to event seems unmotivated by the reality of the characters and their situations. Egri offers the following example of this last form: If a normally upstanding person finds himself needing a new suit, his first solution shouldn't be to rob a bank to get money. Through drama, we can take him on a downward spiral where robbing the bank, an action totally foreign to his previous philosophy, soon becomes his only option.

Transition

Egri also speaks of the importance of *transition*, the idea that characters should be in a constant state of emotional flux. "We are never, for any successive two moments, the same," and our drama should reflect this, as characters experience subtle shifts, feints, and revelations throughout the story that take them from one emotional pole to another. This flux ensures that your conflict will rise and that your characters will grow through the course of the play.

Three Movements

Unlike many of the major screenwriting gurus (and perhaps because his book was not written primarily for screenwriters), Egri keeps the structural rules of his system comparatively loose. He does not mandate formal act breaks or indicate specific places at which certain types of events have to occur in the drama.

The closest Egri comes to providing a structural system is in his definition of a drama's *three movements*, which bear names similar to those provided by fellow writing sage Syd Field (see p. 50–51 for more details).

Egri's Three Movements

The establishment of the conflict leads to a

(1) *CRISIS* in the antagonists' lives, which grows in intensity until the

(2) *CLIMAX*, when everything comes to a head and the two forces meet in their most naked and aggressive opposition. This situation leads naturally to the

(3) *RESOLUTION*, in which the victor emerges from the conflict triumphant, and the premise has been proven.

This order gives you a solid foundation for structure, without straitjacketing you with page-length or running-time requirements.

Egri also maintains (crucially, I might add) that each scene in a play mirrors this crisis-climax-resolution structure, and that the resolution of each minicrisis takes us one step closer to resolving the maxicrisis that results in proving the play's premise.

Dialogue

Naturally, as a playwright, Egri places much greater importance on dialogue than the screenwriting gurus do. Dialogue is, after all, the primary means of conveying information on the stage, and it therefore achieves much more weight than in film, where images carry the burden of the story. Still, if one can remember to think of dialogue as it relates to screenwriting rather than to the stage, Egri passes along some useful nuggets: "Your point will carry further if unhampered by unnecessary verbiage." "Let the man speak in the language of his own world." "Never use your play as your soap box." (Uh, that last one's gonna be tough with characters that exist primarily to prove a premise, but okay.)

Egri provides numerous lengthy examples from plays to prove his dramatic theories. Principally, he cites Moliere's *Tartuffe*, various works by Shakespeare, and especially Ibsen's *A Doll's House* (see p. 99 for a structural analysis of Ibsen's work). The examples are useful, but many of the plays Egri cites, although doubtless widely known to a general reader in 1946, have since passed into obscurity. By the same token, you might as well skip the section at the end on "How to Market a Play"; the biz has changed some since World War Two.

Egri is good, I think, for fine-tuning your script. This is not starter-level stuff, and it won't really help you glean the wheat from the chaff when you're first trying to hammer out a confident structure — but he is a gold mine of useful prescriptions for tightening up your work, and I think his ideas would best be applied in the context of revision.

EXERCISE: LAJOS EGRI

Using the same film you selected for the Aristotle exercise, define, in a simple phrase, the *premise* of the film, as Lajos Egri uses the term.

_____

_____

_____

_____

HOWARD & MABLEY: Ironying Out the Wrinkles

*In the first act, it's who the people are and what is the
situation of this whole story. The second act is the
progression of that situation to a high point of conflict
and great problems. And the third act is how the
conflicts and problems are resolved.*

— Ernest Lehman

WHEN THE NAMES OF EMINENT AUTHORITIES on
screenwriting are bandied about, two that always come up are
David Howard and Edward Mabley. Their bestseller, *The Tools
of Screenwriting: A Writer's Guide to the Craft and Elements of
a Screenplay* (New York: St. Martin's Griffin, 1995), is actually
a book based on a book. Mabley wrote *Dramatic Construction*
about the craft of playwriting in 1972, and twenty years later
Howard revised it into this book on screenwriting. Howard also
incorporates many insights from his mentor, the distinguished
academician Frank Daniel.

These three fellows are heavyweight academics. Howard was
the founding director of the graduate screenwriting program at
the USC School of Cinema-Television (my alma mater). Mabley
was a playwright who taught at the New School for Social Research in New York and died in 1984. Daniel headed up many of
the world's renowned film schools, like the Center for Advanced
Film Studies at the American Film Institute, the Sundance Institute, and the USC Cinema-Television school. (Daniel was at USC
after my time there. The Cinema Department, as it was called in
my day, had only a rudimentary dramatic writing program. If I'd
been there when Daniel was in charge, I'd be writing like Howard
and Mabley, and the book you're reading wouldn't exist.)

This high-minded textbook will not steer you wrong. It is an
elevated discussion of the art and craft of dramatic writing, and
the authors undertake to teach you all kinds of things I wouldn't
presume to touch with a pole... like how to write well. In fact,
their book begins with an explanation of why approaches like
mine are crap. Daniel says in his introduction:

A great many teachers and authors talk about "the three-act structure" rather than about a division of three acts, but the former phrasing gives rise to the implication that the telling of a story is like the building of a bridge... In reality, a story *evolves*; its "structure" changes as the story unfolds; it is constantly in flux. Moreover, there is no fixed structure that works for the telling of a story; each new story is its own prototype, each must be created anew. There is no recipe, there is no blank form that must only have the blanks filled in for a story to take shape. The worst thing a book on screenwriting can do is to instill in the mind of the beginning writer a set of rules, regulations, formulas, prescriptions and recipes... hacks believe in recipes and stick to them anxiously and injudiciously... Professionals, true masters, search for principles.

I must confess that I have a hard time drawing a clear line between hackneyed recipes and masterly principles. In fact, it seems to me that in steering clear of the depravities of "structure," the authors have nevertheless accumulated an awful lot of *rules*. They talk about *premise, theme, objective, obstacles, main tension, third act tension, recognition, revelation,* and *culmination* — all of which would flatten me if I didn't have a really simple and muscular system for utilizing all this.

At no point do they lay out their system schematically, so I will. The words are theirs, but I have crushed them together into one place.

DEFINITION OF CONFLICT
Somebody wants something badly and is having difficulty getting it.

CHARACTER
- The essence of characterization is the revelation of the inner life of the character.

 ❧ *Protagonist & Objective.* The protagonist of a screenplay is usually the main character. The chief characteristic of the protagonist is a desire to achieve a certain goal. The movement toward that *objective* determines where the film shall begin and end.

 ❧ *Obstacle & Antagonist.* The protagonist and his objective constitute the first two elements in the construction of a story; the various *obstacles* collectively constitute the third. When there is a clear-cut opposing character, he or she is known as the antagonist.

 ❧ The main character (protagonist) changes and develops during the second act, or at least intense pressure is put on the character to change, and that change is manifested in the third act.

ACT I:
Introduces the audience to the world of the story and its principal characters, and sets up the main conflict around which the story will be built.

ACT II:
 ❧ Approximately one half of the story and concludes with the *culmination*, which is the high or low point of the screenplay, the event toward which all that precedes is driving.

 ❧ Consists most pressingly and urgently of a series of obstacles, which together are known as the *main tension* and can be summed up as: "Will the protagonist stand up for him/herself?"

 ❧ The main tension is the conflict *solely of Act Two* and is resolved at the culmination, thus creating a new tension, which can be stated as: "What will happen?"

ACT III:
Leads directly (with twists and turns) from the culmination to the *resolution* of the overriding conflict of the entire story.

I'm not going to attempt to summarize this magisterial book beyond the above, but I do want to mention a few points it makes that impressed me as particularly savvy.

Negative Conflict

"Not wanting to do something (or attempting to stop something from happening) is as strong as actively wanting something for the purpose of creating conflict. Trying to get out of a situation or return to a more desirable status quo is wanting something."

Yelling & Screaming

"There is a tendency in the beginning screenwriter to think of conflict as always involving shouting, guns, fists or other forms of extreme behavior… Conflict is created not by histrionics and excessive behavior, but by a character wanting something that is difficult to get or achieve."

An example of what they're talking about can be seen in *The Abyss*, in which Ed Harris and Mary Elizabeth Mastrantonio play a married couple who, to all appearances, hate each other. From their first encounter, they are shouting at and about each other: "They bought you cheap!" "You wiener!" "I hate that bitch!" After watching this action for a while, one realizes that the characters are just treading water, and that the filmmaker is hoping that all this yelling somehow constitutes a conflict.* These two continue to exchange invective until an hour into the picture, at which point it is revealed that they really like each other; this abuse is just their normal level of banter. So, in spite of all the snarling, no genuine conflict is there.

Audience Boredom

"But there must be obstacles to keep the character from achieving easily whatever he or she wants. If it is easy to win the race, paint the picture, or save the life, then the audience says, 'So what?' Audience disinterest is the result of a lack of difficulty to the circumstance."

---

*To avoid attributing deeds and motives to somebody who may or may not be culpable, I will occasionally posit an omnipotent individual called "the filmmaker," who is to be held responsible for everything in the movie.

Hope and Fear

"So what is the trick behind keeping the audience participating in the story and creating in itself the emotional response that drama depends upon? In a word, uncertainty." Another way of putting this idea is: *hope versus fear.* "If the filmmaker can get the audience to *hope* for one turn of events and *fear* another... this state of uncertainty becomes a very powerful tool indeed." Without fear, the audience will be bored; without hope, they'll give up (and early). But yank them back and forth between these emotions and you'll nail them to the edge of their chewing gum–encrusted seats.

Premise

"The premise... is simply the entire situation that exists as the protagonist starts moving toward his objective. This includes all background material pertinent to the story." (*"There's this guy, see, and he..."*) Note that this usage of the word "premise" is altogether different than that employed by Lajos Egri (see pp. 35-37 of this book). *The Tools of Screenwriting*, indeed, outlines an idea very similar to that of Egri's "premise," but calls this concept "Theme" instead.

Subtext

"The (interplay) between what appears to be going on between characters and what is really going on is called subtext." Robert Towne is quoted to the effect that "Most scenes are rarely about what the subject matter is. Most people seldom confront things head-on; they're afraid to. I think that most people try to be accommodating in life, but in back of their accommodation is suppressed fear, or anger, or both."

Dramatic Irony

Howard and Mabley define "dramatic irony" simply as the audience knowing something that the characters don't. I think it's worth our while to spend a little time on the subject of irony, and this place is as good as any. The linguist H. W. Fowler says the following about dramatic irony:

Irony is a form of utterance that postulates a double audience, consisting of one party that hearing shall hear and not understand, and another party that, when more is meant than meets the ear, is aware both of that more and of the outsiders' incomprehension.... The double audience is essential... to what is called *dramatic irony*, i.e., the irony of the Greek drama. That drama had the peculiarity of providing the double audience – one party in the secret and the other not – in a special manner. The facts of most Greek plays were not a matter for invention, but were part of every Athenian child's store of legend; all the spectators, that is, were in the secret beforehand of what would happen.* But the characters, Pentheus and Oedipus and the rest, were in the dark; one of them might utter words that to him and his companions on the stage were of trifling import, but to those who hearing could understand were pregnant with the coming doom. The surface meaning for the dramatis personae, and the underlying one for the spectators; the dramatist working his effect by irony....[12]

Jeremy Campbell, Washington correspondent for *The Evening Standard*, gives us a bit of history on irony:

We humans are in an ironical situation, because we are limited creatures in a universe that has no limits...** We could say that irony is a sort of lie, albeit an out-in-the-open kind of falsehood, useful in a world where reality is very different from appearance and where truth may turn out to be not what it seems. In classical Greece, *eironia* meant a devious way of fooling someone by adopting a false front, or

---

* This knowing is roughly analogous to the contemporary phenomenon of watching a classic film where "everyone" already knows a major narrative twist even before they've seen the film. Can you name anyone who hasn't seen *Star Wars* who *still* doesn't know that Darth Vader is Luke Skywalker's father?

[12] H. W. Fowler, *Dictionary of Modern English Usage* (London: Oxford, 1965), 305–306.

** Not unlike the characters in *Alien*... much to their destruction.

a tricky use of language.... According to the Roman grammarian Donatus in the fourth century A.D., *Ironia est tropus per contrarium quod cognatur ostendens* — "Irony is a trope that shows the opposite of what one perceives." Its medium was incongruity and disparity, which distinguished it from metaphor, a dealer in samenesses. Socratic irony, in which the disingenuous Socrates pretends to need information and professes mock admiration for his intellectual inferiors, was related to the codes of Greek comedy, in which a character simulated humility in order to outwit a boastful but dimwitted confidence trickster...."An irony," according to a seventeenth-century grammarian, "hath the honey of pleasantness in its mouth, and a sting of rebuke in its tail." The term "irony" came into popular use in the eighteenth century and meant saying the opposite of what you mean, intending a strong opinion by voicing a weak one. In all its various manifestations, irony implies that a speaker or writer wants to keep truth at arm's length, for one reason or another....[13]

Character

Earlier I expressed dissatisfaction with Howard and Mabley's definition of characterization as "the revelation of the inner life of the character," not because it wasn't true, but because I found it lacking analytical specificity, and therefore difficult to put to use. How am I, as a writer, to go about putting this revelation on the page? What techniques can I marshal to move these inner secrets out of the character's interior and onto the screen?

Howard and Mabley offer one character precept that is happily explicit: *Intense pressure is put on the character to change during the second act, and that change is manifested in the third act*, otherwise stated as: *Will the main character stand up for him/herself?* This question is one you can work with.

---

[13] Jeremy Campbell, *The Liar's Tale: A History of Falsehood* (New York: W.W. Norton, 2001), 146–150.

EXERCISE: HOWARD & MABLEY

In your previously selected film, locate three instances in which the screenplay utilizes dramatic irony, as defined by Howard and Mabley. Name three moments in the film in which the audience knows something that the characters don't.

1. _____
2. _____
3. _____

SYD FIELD: Brother, Can You Paradigm?

*A structural approach to screenwriting requires patience
and discipline, but the rewards are great. You might find
if you spend three weeks hammering out your story,
the actual screenwriting will take only a week.*

— Greg Marcks

ONE OF HOLLYWOOD'S CONTEMPORARY MAVENS of screenwriting is Syd Field, whose book *Screenplay: The Foundations of Screenwriting* (latest edition © 2005 by Delta, New York) is arguably the best-known scriptwriting manual on the market today. Field is a household name among screenwriting students and has accumulated a lot of respect within the industry as well. The back cover of his book features endorsements from major industry names, including award-winning writers like Steven Bochco (*NYPD Blue*) and James L. Brooks (*Terms of Endearment, The Simpsons*).

Screenplay is an uplifting exposition of the screenwriter's craft. Field, unlike Yr. Present Embittered Scrivener, is no cynic, which may contribute to his book's popularity. "When you create your screenplay," Field enthuses, "you've accomplished a tremendous achievement... It's a satisfying and rewarding experience. You did what you set out to do.

"Wear that proudly. Talent is God's gift," he gushes. "Either you've got it, or you don't. But that doesn't interfere with the experience of writing. Writing brings its own rewards. Enjoy them."

Field credentials himself by discussing his stint as development executive for Cinemobile, a company that pioneered the "one-truck" concept of film production. During that time, Field read more than 2,000 screenplays. (The mind reels.) He also taught a class at Gary Shusett's sadly defunct Sherwood Oaks Experimental College — an honor I share with him, although Field taught writing, and I taught acting for the screen. Sherwood Oaks was, as Field says, "the most unique film school in the country," where the likes of Dustin Hoffman, Martin Scorsese, and William Fraker taught their respective disciplines. Shusett was, and remains, a considerable talent, and so is his brother Ronnie, with whom I wrote *Alien* and *Total Recall*.

Written with the raw beginner in mind, *Screenplay* tells you how to format a script, what a shot is, and so forth. "When you complete this book," Field promises, "you will know exactly what to do to write a screenplay." Fair enough.

Field calls his screenwriting methodology "The Paradigm." "Paradigm" means "model or pattern."* In Field's usage, "The Paradigm" refers to a particular way of thinking about screenplays. The Paradigm is an all-inclusive compilation of conventional wisdom about screenwriting: a great gathering-together of time-honored rules and heuristics, patterned into a kind of consensus of everything that has ever been said about dramatic writing.

In its simplest iteration, The Paradigm is, like the screenwriting form espoused by Howard and Mabley, a three-act system.

Act One: Setup

Act One, "The Setup," introduces the main characters and lays out the particulars of the story, as well as establishing what Field calls the "dramatic situation," by which he means the details of the world the characters inhabit (time period, political realities, economic situation, etc.). In this act, you also establish

---

* "Paradigm," in the original Greek, meant "the inflections of nouns, verbs or other parts of speech."

your main character's "dramatic need," defined as what the character hopes to "win, gain, get or achieve" during the course of the story.

Act Two: Confrontation

Act Two, "The Confrontation," presents your character with numerous "obstacles" he must overcome in order to realize his need. Field: "If you know the character's dramatic need, you can create obstacles to that need. How he overcomes his obstacles is your story." One issue he does not address is whether the obstacles should escalate in intensity as the story progresses (a subject I will be discussing in great detail in Chapter Ten). One would assume this trajectory to be the wise course of action for the storyteller, though Field never comes out and says so. Otherwise, you may find your story treading water as your hero faces a series of interchangeable, equally surmountable obstacles, or (if you're in the hands of a unusually perverse screenwriter) they might find things actually getting easier for them as the story progresses.

Act Three: Resolution

In Act Three, "The Resolution," loose ends are tied up and the plot is brought to its conclusion in the way that the previous action indicates. Field stresses that "resolution" does not mean "happy ending," but rather an ending that is appropriate to the story you have chosen to tell, and he cites several examples of successful films with downbeat or ambiguous endings that are still dramatically satisfying. In particular, he references Robert Towne's screenplay for *Chinatown*, which ends with a bleak, nihilistic final scene that is nonetheless consistent with everything that has gone before.* Field actually cites *Chinatown* a lot (it's referenced thirty-four times in *Screenplay's* index, and Chapter Seven of the book is an in-depth analysis of the first ten pages of Towne's script), so if you are planning to read Field's book and

---

*Field does remind us that Towne's original ending was more traditionally upbeat, and that the finale only took on its darker cast after Roman Polanski signed on as *Chinatown's* director.

haven't seen the film yet, you might want to check it out first. Honestly, you should probably just see it regardless. It's a hell of a movie.

Plot Points

Field divides his three acts into units of length that have a little flexibility, but not much. Using a 120-page screenplay as a model (Field subscribes to the "one-page-equals-one-minute" school of screenwriting), he states that Act One should be "approximately" thirty pages in length; Act Two, sixty; Act Three, thirty. The act breaks are determined by what Field calls "plot points," defined as "any event that 'hooks' into the action and spins it around in another direction." Needless to say, there are a number of plot points throughout a screenplay. Really, any time your characters enter a different location or meet a new character, the action has "spun" to some degree. Field concedes that a writer is free to use as many plot points as his script requires. But, this being the case, how do we know which crucial plot points mark the act breaks? One might be forgiven for harboring a suspicion that the plot points at the end of Acts One and Two are "crucial" simply because they come after the correct number of pages, but any sense that these plot points carry any greater dramatic weight than the others is merely implied by Field.

Character Bios

Despite all the emphasis on structure, Field maintains that "action and character" are the true cornerstones of a solid screenplay. He recommends constructing character biographies before you begin work on a script. Your main character's life should be divided into an "interior" life — a description of everything that has happened to the character prior to the screenplay's action (birth, childhood, schooling) — and an "exterior," the action we see during the course of the film. This "exterior" is likewise divided into three subgroups: *professional*, *personal* (relationship issues), and *private* (opinions, beliefs, and tastes). These capsule histories will help you assemble fleshed-out characters. Field also states that character is a "point of view," "attitude," "personality," "behavior," "revelation," and "identification." The basic idea: Character is complicated.

SCREENPLAY IS FULL OF FIELD-COINED TERMINOL-OGY, charts and diagrams depicting his theoretical constructs, and oft-repeated mantras designed to drill his core concepts into the reader's head. For example, if you flip through the book, you'll find the phrase KNOW YOUR ENDING! all over the place. Field asserts that all scripts must have forward momentum in order to hold viewer interest, and that for the writer to create this sense of confident direction, the ending of the script must be known in advance — before your fingers even touch the keyboard. Therefore... KNOW YOUR ENDING!

Likewise, just as he stresses the importance of knowing your ending, Field emphasizes the necessity of a good beginning, in particular your script's crucial first ten pages. During his tenure with Cinemobile, Field read numerous screenplays that failed to grab him within the first ten pages. Because he was always backlogged with a huge stack of scripts to read, he couldn't afford to waste time on a sub-par script, so any screenplay that wasn't going anywhere by page 10 went in Field's "maybe file" (read: wastebasket). It's a reminder of the harsh reality of the Hollywood marketplace, and that no writer should give a reader any excuse not to read his script. Hence, those first ten pages become decisive in hooking the reader and getting him to stick with your script to the end.

Field also spends a great deal of time discussing "context" and "content," though he never makes it clear exactly what these devices are about. It appears from the surrounding text that "context" is really the same thing as the "dramatic situation" mentioned before (i.e., the details of the world the characters inhabit). "Content" is really just the action of the story. Field invents additional terms for us to keep track of, then complicates things further by drawing the repeated analogy of the *context* as the inside of a cup that holds the *content* together. Field admits that these are "abstract principles" at best, so you'll likely find yourself flipping back to his initial outlining of the concepts every time they come up.

Screenplay styles itself as a one-stop source of screenwriting knowledge, but in my estimation, this should be more of a first stop. Field does a good job delineating numerous aspects of screenplay structural theory and illustrates them with strong examples from well-known films, but the book attempts to cover so much ground in a relatively short space (the latest edition of *Screenplay*, sans table of contents and index, runs a brisk 309 pages) that certain concepts naturally get short shrift or remain nebulous conceptual sketches. My advice: After reading Field's book, seek out other sources for additional information on any of Field's concepts that seem especially important or problematic to you.

EXERCISE: SYD FIELD

Does your chosen film conform to the "Paradigm" of three-act structure, as defined by Syd Field? If so, how far into the film do the act breaks occur, and when do the major "plot points" happen? If not, does the film still use conventional act breaks, and if so, when in the narrative do they occur?

ROBERT MCKEE: Falling Into The Gap

*What I adore is supreme professionalism. I'm bored
by writers who can only write when it is raining.*

— Noel Coward

SURE, SYD FIELD IS A BIG NAME in the how-to screenwriting game. But has he ever been a character in an Oscar-winning movie? Robert McKee has (in Spike Jonze and Charlie Kaufman's *Adaptation*, where he was played by British thespian Brian Cox). As of this writing, McKee is the *au courant* screenwriting guru,* and his hefty how-to book *Story: Substance, Structure, Style and the Principles of Screenwriting* (New York: It Books, 1997) is *the* must-read for writers, executives, and development personnel. McKee teaches screenwriting seminars in Los Angeles, New York, and Europe, and he serves as consultant to several production companies. His bio tells us that "his credits include numerous television and feature films." (No production names are given, perhaps for contractual reasons, nor are there any indications of McKee's role on these projects). Like Field, McKee fills the back cover of his book with endorsements from industry names. TV writer Dennis Dugan (*Hill Street Blues*) calls McKee "the Stanislavski of writing," and Kirk Douglas says, "He not only teaches, he inspires."

McKee's vision of Hollywood is one of the rosiest I've ever encountered. "If you show a brilliant, original screenplay to agents," McKee says, "they'll fight for the right to represent you. The agent you hire will incite a bidding war among story-starved producers, and the winner will pay you an embarrassing amount of money. What's more, once in production, your *finished* screenplay will meet with surprisingly little interference." Phew... now that's a Hollywood *I* want to work in.

In his introduction, McKee speaks of "archetypes, not stereotypes," and says that writing is about "mastering the art, not

---

*In the interest of full disclosure, I should mention that McKee's book speaks well of me and of *Alien*, so I don't dare give him a bad write-up, for fear of charges of ingratitude.

second-guessing the marketplace." He invokes Kenneth Burke's oft-quoted dictum about stories as "equipment for living," designed to help us determine the hidden patterns and narratives in our own lives. Still, he downplays the role of art in storytelling, saying that poetry has no place in a screenplay. According to McKee, 75% of the writer's job is laying out the story's structure, which he defines as "a selection of events from the characters' life stories that is composed into a strategic sequence to arouse specific emotions and to express a specific view of life." Those events are the basic building blocks of everything that comes after, dictating changes in the lives of the characters that are expressed in terms of *values*. These values are central to McKee's concept of storytelling, and can change from positive to negative or vice versa from moment to moment, giving the story a dramatically satisfying rhythm. Naturally, like Field and Egri, McKee insists that the changes needed to express these values can only be reached through *conflict*, a character's reaction to the challenges the story places in his path.

Beat, Scene, Sequence

Several components make up the body of a completed screen story as McKee envisions it. The smallest unit is a "beat," which is basically just a moment of action or behavior between characters. These "beats" are structured into scenes, "extended conflict-driven actions" that somehow transform a character's values at particular points in the story. Ideally, McKee says, every scene in the script should constitute one of these story events, changing the lives of the characters in perhaps irreversible ways: "The goal is no scene that doesn't turn." He maintains that there should be "forty to sixty scenes" in the average film, arranged in sequences that impact the changing values of the characters more greatly than any of the scenes could on their own. McKee actually recommends titling your sequences while developing your script, to keep each sequence's function straight in your mind during the process.

Acts and More Acts

The sequences are likewise shaped into acts, which peak with the major changes the characters undergo in the course of their journey through the conflicts of the story. McKee believes that three acts are the *minimum* a film can contain and still present a viable dramatic story, but he by no means thinks that three acts are the be-all of screenplay structure. In his estimation, a story should contain "as many acts as it needs." (Although it may be technically true, this advice represents a failure to understand the power of three acts and the weakening effect of additional acts; more on this in Chapter Eleven.) He breaks down a few multi-act films to demonstrate his hypothesis; *Four Weddings and a Funeral* turns out to have a "Shakespearean" five-act structure,* whereas *The Cook, The Thief, His Wife and Her Lover* spreads its story over a whopping *eight* acts. (But, as McKee himself points out, it is almost impossible to make this kind of thing really work.)

Regardless of the number of acts, McKee feels that all film stories contain basically five essential components.

The *Inciting Incident*, which should come in the first 25% of the screenplay, "radically upsets the balance of forces in the protagonist's life," driving him to start taking action to rectify this problem and restore that balance.

As the story goes on, *Progressive Complications* pile up, pushing the protagonist away from his chosen goal or toward a new, unexpected goal that he has only recognized through the course of the story.

Then, customarily near the end of the screenplay, the *Crisis* arrives, a deliberately static moment where the character reaches the crucial choice he must make during the course of the story, to turn back and save himself further anguish, or press ahead,

---

*I feel obligated to point out that while Shakespeare is our greatest genius of character, he is mediocre at plot construction. For example, to experience the most contrived ending in known history, check out *Romeo and Juliet*. I'm talking about that business with the potion/poison, which Shakespeare cobbles together to get R&J each to think that the other is dead. The contrivance ultimately doesn't matter, of course, because the character beats overpower any considerations of plausibility. But still...

for good or ill, to try to achieve his goal and restore balance to his world. This moment is McKee's "Obligatory Scene," which all of the preceding action of the script has been building to, and although not necessarily the action peak of the story, this scene is the emotional high point.

The action motivated by the Crisis takes us to the *Climax*, which can come either right on the heels of the Crisis (like Thelma and Louise driving off that cliff mere seconds after deciding to do so) or follow a series of rising actions motivated by the decision made at the moment of Crisis (*Casablanca's* third-act twists are a good example of this, which we'll examine in detail in the structural analysis in Chapter Seven.)

The Climax thus takes us to the *Resolution*, which can be positively or negatively charged, or ironically intermingle both values in a "realistic" fashion. Like Field and Egri — and anybody else with any common sense — McKee believes that a film does not have to have a "happy" ending, just a Resolution that satisfactorily ties up everything that has preceded it. He also believes that every film contains a "Controlling Idea" (analogous to Egri's "premise") that is summed up by the Resolution's value orientation. Love conquers or destroys all, man or fate is the master of all action, and so forth. However, unlike Egri, McKee believes that this Controlling Idea emerges naturally as a screenwriter creates the story, rather than the writer crafting a story around a notion he wishes to prove. McKee's idea here is closer to my own way of thinking. (In *Alien*, once I started writing, I got the idea that the Ripley character would err [wisely] on the side of caution, while the John Hurt character would [foolishly] take bold risks, and that the story, as it played out, would show caution to be the path of wisdom. But I didn't make the movie to prove that point!)

Archplot, Miniplot, Antiplot

Perhaps owing to his looser conception of act structure, McKee also eschews the frequent desire of many screenwriting instructors to attempt to wrench every story into the classical Hollywood narrative mold, what he describes as the "Arch-plot," in which the hero faces the bad guy in a temporally and spatially unambiguous world where the good are rewarded and the villainous punished "in a closed ending of absolute, irreversible change." The majority of commercial films, from *Casablanca* and *Annie Hall* to *Pearl Harbor*, falls into this mold. However, McKee also acknowledges "Miniplot" films with multiple, usually passive protagonists, primarily internal conflicts, and frequently open endings. Ensemble films like *The Big Chill* and *The Breakfast Club* are examples of this type. He even explains the "Antiplot," which dispenses with reality altogether, giving us inconsistent worlds, nonlinear time, and largely coincidence-driven narrative. This type is frequently the realm of experimental filmmakers, and includes such works as *Last Year at Marienbad*, *After Hours*, even *Monty Python and the Holy Grail*. McKee maintains that, though Archplot films dominate the marketplace, writers must ultimately determine for themselves what form works best for their storytelling sensibilities and focus their energies there.

Object of Desire

Of course, regardless of plot, form, or genre (which McKee writes a good bit about, including a long list in which he lays out — gasp! — *25 different genres*), story still gives us *character* and *conflict* as the ultimate soul of drama. Character, namely the protagonist, is important to McKee's story concept because it is within the protagonist that a story's "Center of Good" resides. Regardless of whether he is a "good" person, a protagonist should contain the core positive values of the story, the values that drive us through the narrative and are tested by the conflicts the story throws in the protagonist's path. The "spine" of every screenplay is the protagonist's quest for his object of desire, and in effectively constructed screenplays, the urge for this object is double-tiered; the object of the protagonist's *conscious* desire also symbolizes something the character *unconsciously* desires. This unconscious need often contradicts the conscious desire and frequently supplants it in importance as the character moves toward the Climax. In short, it's a conflict between what a character *wants* and what he merely *thinks* he wants. *Casablanca*, a film we will discuss in detail later, provides an excellent example of this duality, in which the protagonist's conscious desire to be left alone with his self-pity begins to give way to his unconscious desire to do the right thing — virtually from the moment that his former paramour walks into his gin joint.

The quest for this "object of desire" inevitably brings the protagonist into conflict. The forces of antagonism arrayed against your character must be suitably strong and imposing. McKee says, "A protagonist and his story can only be as intellectually fascinating and emotionally compelling as the forces of antagonism make them." If your character's obstacles are too easily surmountable, or so powerful that victory over him is impossible, your story will lose narrative momentum and turn into a fast drive down a dead-end street. After the "Inciting Incident," which enters your character into conflict, he will embark on a series of actions that will create shifting positive and negative values in the film's world as the character advances toward his goal. According to McKee, to be most effective, conflict must exist on three levels: *personal*, *extra-personal*, and *internal*. In other words, the most effective dramatic hero is simultaneously at war with other people, with the world, and with himself.

The Gap

True cinematic drama ultimately resides in what McKee describes as "The Gap." Every time a character takes an action, according to McKee, he has an expectation of what will happen as a result. To create dramatic tension and interest, there must be a substantial "gap" between the character's expectation and his action's result, a gap that suspends or prevents the immediate achievement of his goal and requires him to take additional actions, thus opening more and wider expectation/result gaps. The hero's goal becomes to close these "gaps," thus unifying expectation and result. Once this merging occurs, the hero's actions will have the desired effect — the drama will be resolved, and the hero will achieve his goal. Of course, this resolution happens in different ways for Miniplot and Antiplot films, but for the most part, McKee gears his theoretical material toward the Archplot, the standard Hollywood narrative archetype.

There's a lot of material in *Story* that you will find in Egri, Field, and the numerous other screenwriting how-to-ers. Like all the rest, McKee recommends using index cards to map out your story sequences;* espouses the importance of research, treatments, character bios, and the like in fleshing out your story; warns against relying too heavily on dialogue in film, and so on. Considering all of this essentially duplicated material, what exactly has given *Story* such an exalted reputation, such cachet, elevated it over Field, Egri et al. as the number one screenwriting manual for the Hollywood intelligentsia?

Well, McKee writes with verve on every single aspect of screenplay construction. There is nothing, down to the finest detail, for which he is unable to come up with a rule. So, if comprehensive coverage is what you're looking for in a screenwriting book, McKee is your man.

Or maybe it's just the *diagrams*. Hollywood is a town run not by artists, but by number-crunchers, and artistic principles will be easier for them to digest if they're presented in a form with which they're already familiar: flowcharts, pie charts, graphs and the like. McKee's book is stuffed with these, over three dozen by my count, illustrating everything from the "Three Levels of Conflict" to the proprietary "Gap" concept. Although some readers feel that these diagrams needlessly complicate otherwise easily understood concepts, the Hollywood bean counters

---

*For the record, I've never used an index card.

no doubt breathe a sigh of relief. At last! The elusive art of storytelling graphed out in quantifiable, clip-n-save diagram form! McKee, in short, knows how to present his ideas in the language of the money man.

Don't ignore *Story's* page count as a potential secret of its success, either. It's longer than any other dramatic writing book I've come across. The main text alone, not including film lists and indexes, runs (count 'em) *419 pages*. Everybody knows that in Hollywood, bigger is better, and *Story's* sheer bulk, as much as its ideas, may have contributed to its reputation as the authoritative screenwriting book.

EXERCISE: ROBERT MCKEE

Provide three examples from your chosen film of the screenplay's usage of McKee's "gaps." What does the hero hope to accomplish through these three actions, and what is the difference between his expectation and the action's actual result?

1. _____

_____

2. _____

_____

3. _____

_____

WHAT WE HAVE SEEN from examining these books is that they all teach the same basic method, cast in different terms. Each author has his own take on dramatic structure; behind the varying terminology and details, they all describe what amounts to the same thing, the same way of putting together a story. It's evolved over generations, a centuries-long process in which the most effective way to tell stories to audiences has been discovered by painful trial and error. Of course, the devil, as they say, is in the details, and that is where these writers find their respective niches.

But enough about other people's systems, already. From this point on, we'll be talking about my system, a.k.a. *Dynamic Structure*.

The difference between traditional screenplay structural systems and my own (as we are going to see) is that mine is a *specific case of the general method*. Some obvious similarities exist between the traditional method and mine. Both are based on *conflict*, both employ a *three-act structure*, both place special emphasis on the *end of the second act*, and both *resolve* the screenplay's particular primary conflict. The difference between the two systems is that they utilize (1) *different definitions of dramatic conflict*, and (2) *different conceptions of what happens at the end of the second act*. The general definition of conflict is "a protagonist's struggle to attain a desired goal"; *my* definition of conflict is "a dispute over an issue." This difference allows me (and any writer who uses my system) to render conflict as a rounded, two-sided phenomenon, rather than as a version of one-character-versus-whatever, and it is based on the psychological principle that nothing is more arresting to an observer than a knock-down, drag-out fight. Also, the traditional second-act curtain is the "high point of the story" — mine is "the escalation of the conflict to a point of irreversibility."

The traditional approach, in short, is *striving-based*.

Mine is ***fight-based***.

Chapter Four

Dynamic Conflict Defined,
or Guy Versus Guy

*What's the conflict that will tell
the story you want to tell?*

— Walter Bernstein

MANY THINGS MAY HAPPEN. Many things are interesting. But not all things, even interesting things, are *dramatic*. **DRAMA IS CONFLICT**. Simply put, without conflict, there can be no drama. Without conflict, there is boredom.

An old storytelling saw contends that the three-act structure is as simple as "Put a man up a tree; throw stones at the man; get the man down." But "a man up a tree" is not truly conflict, unless something has *forced* him up the tree. Conflict occurs *between characters* and consists of a controversy over something: *an issue of contention*. The characters must disagree over how to address this issue, and their running disagreement constitutes the body of the story. The action arises from the characters' interference with each other as they attempt to resolve the issue in directly contradictory ways. The technical term in Greek tragedy was *agon*. And it all boils down to one simple question: *Who will prevail?*

Conflict is what your story is really about. Not, "My story is about a guy who is a cowboy." Not, "My story is about two people who fall in love." Not, "My story is about the futility of modern life." Those are premises, themes, setups, whatever you want to call them. Your story is about *conflict*. If it's not, it shouldn't even dignify itself with the name "story."

Precisely what the conflict is about — the "issue" between the characters — is ultimately unimportant. That's why it is impossible to think of an inherently boring subject for a movie. Like, say, philately. Some people might think that a movie about stamp collecting would be colossally boring. Some people might be right. But such a movie wouldn't be boring if I wrote it, because it wouldn't be about stamp collecting at all. It would be about fear and desire and *conflict*, and conflict is always interesting. Always. People's eyes are inherently attracted to conflict. Two dogs start fighting; everyone stops to watch. Few things get our adrenaline pumping faster than a brawl. The fact that the characters in my hypothetical story would be in conflict over postage stamps would be incidental. They could be in conflict over fingernail clippings. Long story short, if you wish to tell a story about stamps or loose fingernails or whatever, you damn well better find a *conflict* that illustrates what you want to say about stamps or fingernails, and then tell the story of that conflict.

So, if someone asks you what your story is about, your answer is, or at least had better be, "My story is about conflict."

THERE ARE THREE KINDS OF CONFLICT:

- *Conflict between characters.* Man versus man. This conflict is the most common type found in storytelling, and (or possibly because) it is the easiest to write.

- *Conflict between man and non-man* ("*The Other*"). Man versus a bear in the woods. Man versus a fire. Man versus a monster from outer space. A man may conflict with an animal, a force of nature, even an inanimate object, but to qualify as dramatic conflict, that object must be treated, in the context of the conflict, as a *character*. The chair a man stumbles over must be given a personality, and a motive for tripping him. This scenario is traditionally referred to as the "pathetic (or affective) fallacy," and it may be a logical fallacy, but it is essential to any dramatic conflict between man and the nonhuman. For an excellent sustained example of this, see *Jaws*, or for a nice microcosm of the concept, watch Jimmy Stewart in *It's a Wonderful Life* as he battles that pesky banister knob that comes loose in his hand again and again.

⁓ *Man versus himself.* Here, the conflict is within one person, between warring aspects of his/her character: *Dr. Jekyll and Mr. Hyde*, *The Lost Weekend*, *Hamlet*. Tragedies generally fall into this category, because in tragedy, as it's classically defined, the main character brings about his or her own downfall.

Multiple Conflicts

Most films utilize multiple conflicts, and it's not uncommon for a single film to boast all three types of conflict and to include more than one instance of at least one of the three types. Which conflict is your screenplay's *main* conflict is a question of emphasis, and it is a decision you will make when engineering your script. But you must make certain that at least one of your conflicts plays all the way through the screenplay, from start to finish.

Another Version of Conflict

As we've seen, some authorities describe "conflict" as something happening to one character (for example, see Howard and Mabley's definition of conflict on p. 43). This definition violates my whole understanding of what conflict is, in common usage as well as in dramaturgy. *Conflict is a contest between somebody and somebody else*, even if one "somebody" is really a group of people (as in *Alien*) or if those conflicting "somebodies" are embodiments of opposing sides of a single person (as in *Jekyll and Hyde*).

The underlying basis of this particular piece of advice from the traditional system — that "conflict" happens to a single character — seems to be that conflict takes place between a character and "obstacles" in his path. Well, that's fine… so long as the obstacles — whatever they are — have personalities and motives of their own.

Conflict, at its core, is a *transaction*.

EXERCISES: DYNAMIC CONFLICT DEFINED

Select three films, each of which utilizes as its principal conflict a different one of the three types of conflict defined in this chapter.

Conflict Between Characters _____

Conflict Between Man and Non-man _____

Man Versus Himself _____

Choosing one of the films listed above, provide examples of how that film utilizes each of the three types of conflict within its screenplay.

Conflict Between Characters _____

_____

Conflict Between Man and Non-man _____

_____

Man Versus Himself _____

_____

Chapter Five

DAN O'BANNON'S DYNAMIC STRUCTURE,
or Getting to Poof

Okay, buckle your seat belts. Here it comes. . .

> — From the screenplay for
> *Terminator 2: Judgment Day,*
> written by James Cameron
> and William Wisher

A MOVIE OF FEATURE LENGTH should be divided into three acts.

Act One *defines* the conflict.

Act Two *elaborates* that conflict to a Point of No Return.

Act Three *resolves* the conflict, for good or ill.

Act One

In Act One, we introduce the characters and their situation. Who, where, when, why. From this conglomeration of people, places, ideas, and desires arises an "issue of contention." The principal characters — the antagonists — differ on how best to deal with the "issue." *As a result, a "conflict" emerges.*

The moment the conflict materializes, Act One is over. The first-act curtain represents the locking of the conflict.

Act Two

Act Two develops the consequences of the conflict until they reach a Point of No Return. Traditionally, Act Two is said to be where "the plot thickens," or — to put it another way — *Act Two takes the antagonists from bad to worse.*

The Point of No Return

The Point of No Return is the moment when the conflict escalates to a level at which a *decisive confrontation* between the opposed characters can no longer be avoided.

You've no doubt heard some situation described as a "comedy of errors." This set-up means that, as a result of some initial folly, circumstances get progressively complicated and difficult until events reach an extremity of ridiculousness. This situation is essentially what you're trying to achieve in all storytelling, even if you're not writing a comedy. When a conflict arises between characters, it's naturally going to lead to them *doing something about it*. That something will lead to another thing, which will lead to yet another... a causal chain of events. That's what I mean when I say that Act Two "develops the consequences of the conflict." As one thing piles on top of another, the situation gets steadily more problematic until it reaches critical mass, a point of irreversibility.

When the antagonists reach The Point of No Return, their freedom of choice evaporates, poof. Prior to this moment, they were free to walk away from the conflict if they felt like it. They just didn't. But that freedom of escape no longer exists, because they've frittered or flung it away.* Their allowable courses of action have narrowed to just one: *decisive confrontation*. All doors slam shut except that one (because they've slammed all the others); they can no longer withdraw, they're stuck on a path with no U-turns and only one exit. The Point of No Return, in short, is the moment when something that they started at the end of Act One finally goes too far and locks them into an inevitable showdown. The Point of No Return is a crisis that ups the ante. It *raises the stakes to the ultimate extreme*. Now the whole intractable mess is going to be, *must be*, settled once and for all, like it or not, devil take the hindmost. To the death.

---

* Yes, they have a *choice*, but even if they vacillate, they're always going to choose to *continue to engage*. If this sounds contrived to you, I invite you to write a screenplay in which your characters choose to *walk away* from their conflict. Let me know how that works out for you... if you can stay awake while you're writing it.

The Point of No Return is what most traditional systems refer to as "the second-act curtain." It is the most important moment in the story, the story's most serious crisis, the turning point. It is also the single most artificial and contrived moment in the story, and the most difficult to write, because at this point, all your story threads must converge. Of course, all fictional plots depend, to a certain degree, on coincidence and improbability. It is, in fact, a carefully chosen improbability that creates the situation that allows high drama to exercise its revelatory vision of human nature.

The Point of No Return defines the story. If you can succinctly describe your Point of No Return, you've told your story. The rest — how the antagonists got there in the first place and how the dust settles afterward — is embroidery.

Act Three

Act Three resolves the conflict, for good or for ill. The moment the conflict is resolved, the story is over. If you feel like it, you can add an epilogue to your story. An epilogue may help to ease the audience out of the movie's spell, or to reassure them that the story has not ended too abruptly, but it is by no means absolutely necessary.

SOME OF MY STUDENTS HAVE TOLD ME they have difficulty figuring out what to write in Act Two. How do you "thicken a plot"?

Look at it this way. If you have your first-act curtain — who's conflicting over what — and you know what your second-act curtain is going to be (because you've figured it out in advance, as you should), then your second act should practically write itself. You know what your conflict is; you know what your Point of No Return is going to be. Those two points are like the ends of a clothesline. Now you just have to run the line between them.

But *how* do you get from one to the other? Well, getting from a conflict to an irreversible escalation of that conflict can seldom be done in a single step; it usually requires an extended series of actions and reactions from the characters in order to compound the conflict into an irreversible condition. *Each action and/or reaction is a scene.* (If your conflict can be escalated in a single step, you'll wind up with an extremely short story — a two-act story, in fact, which I'll discuss in just a moment.) If you just figure out what actions the characters have to take to achieve that escalation, you'll find, at the end of this string of incidents, that you've got your Act Two.

One Act, Two Acts, Five Acts

Stories, of course, do not exist solely in three-act forms. There are one- and two-act forms as well. The short story, a literary form, usually has only one act (not to be confused with novellas and novelettes, which are also called short stories but possess more than one act). There are also one-act stage plays, like Edward Albee's *Zoo Story*, but it is almost impossible to find this form in film or television. A half-hour television episode, for example, has two acts. The clearest example of this structure is the old *Alfred Hitchcock Presents* anthology series, in which a first act of ten to fourteen minutes was spent setting up the situation and a second act of eight to twelve minutes was the meat of the thriller. Just before the station break, the conflict would crystallize, capturing the audience so it stayed tuned for the second half, the "good part" where the narrative trap set in the first act would be sprung and the Hitchcockian twist would hit us with full force.

In essence, this form omits the second act of the standard three-act form. With only two acts to work with, the defining of the conflict and The Point of No Return fuse together into one moment. In other words, the conflict is irreversible at the moment it arises. (That's probably why so many *Alfred Hitchcock Presents* half-hours featured a murder at the end of the first act. Not many actions are more irreversible than taking someone else's life.) The one-act form, by contrast, can be thought of as consisting only of the events of a story's third act. You begin with the characters already in the midst of their major crisis; The Point of No Return becomes sort of the jumping-off point for the whole story.

There are also four-act forms and stories with even more acts, though I personally can't speak to how the internal dynamics of such structures would operate. (We will nevertheless be discussing Shakespeare's typical five-act structure in our Chapter Seven analysis of *King Lear.*) Robert McKee touches on these multi-act constructions (*Story*, p. 220–221), but he likewise doesn't explain exactly how to use them or make them work.

To the best of my understanding, when you move beyond three acts, you lessen your ability to meaningfully escalate your conflict. The act breaks become mere narrative high points, not genuine escalations, which is as good a reason as any to stick with three acts. Not that your story shouldn't have high points between your conflict escalations, but why kid yourself by calling them acts? (We'll get into this subject in even greater detail in Chapter Eleven.)

EXERCISES: DAN O'BANNON'S DYNAMIC STRUCTURE
In your favorite film, what moment would you consider to be the "first-act curtain," the moment when the conflict is defined? What is the "issue" over which the antagonists come into conflict?

_____

_____

_____

_____

_____

What would you say is the film's Point of No Return, the moment at which the conflict reaches its ultimate escalation and becomes irreversible? Define the film's story in one sentence utilizing The Point of No Return as its key moment.

_____

_____

_____

_____

_____

How does the film's conflict resolve itself in the third act? Is the conflict followed through to the absolute end of the story? Does the film feature an epilogue following the resolution of the conflict?

_____

_____

_____

_____

_____

Chapter Six

DYNAMIC CHARACTER: O'BANNON ON CHARACTER AS STRUCTURE,

or Choosy Writers Choose Choice

*Before I write down one word, I must have the character
in my mind through and through. I must penetrate into
the last wrinkle of his soul.*

— Henrik Ibsen

THIS BOOK IS ABOUT STRUCTURE, and character really isn't a structural issue, but it's important enough to the screenwriter to merit our addressing one or two structural prescriptions useful in character development. The word *development*, after all, is time related. It is an indication of the fact that something is happening throughout the scope of the story, and is therefore connected to the structure.

Writers (and those who criticize them) have an attitude toward character that verges on the superstitious. It is considered axiomatic in writerly circles that character is the most important thing in storytelling, and that good characters are the *sine qua non* of good writing. Characterization is held to be an absolute that brooks no denial. To Anthony Burgess, "The convolutions of the human personality, under the stress of artfully selected experience, are the chief fascination" of writing,[14] and even Lajos Egri, for all his talk about premise, regards character as "the

---

[14] Anthony Burgess on "The Novel," from the 15th edition of the Encyclopedia Britannica, available online at http://www.britannica.com/EBcheckedtopic/421071/novel

most interesting phenomenon anywhere." And yet, as William Burroughs points out:

> Some very great writers like Beckett have only one charac-
> ter and need no others... Beckett is quite literally inhuman.
> You will look in vain for human motivations of jealousy,
> hate or love. Even fear is absent. Nothing remains of human
> emotions except weariness and distress, tinged with remote
> sadness...There are no characters as such, and certainly no
> character development. He is perhaps the purest writer who
> ever lived.[15]

Also, as we discussed earlier, Aristotle subordinated character to plot, or at least he thought he did. For Aristotle, "Dramatists do not employ action in order to achieve character portrayal, they include character because of its relation to action." But because the purpose of action is *the revelation of character*, Aristotle — to put it bluntly — is hopelessly confused.

And then there is the special case of science fiction. In "pure" science fiction, character is subordinate to the *idea*. What science fiction is about, for example, is *What if the laws of physics changed?* You can see that this statement has no human referent other than the potential impact of this stated change on people. Science fiction is idea driven instead of character driven, which is why critics and *litterateurs* have traditionally considered it a debased form of writing.* But it's there, and if you're going to write it, you may as well know how to do so effectively. So in "pure" science fiction, if character is developed without reference to the *idea* that is the center of the story, then you will find that the better and more richly developed the character, the worse it will

---

[15] William S. Burroughs, *The Adding Machine: Selected Essays* (New York: Arcade Publishing, 1986), 33, 183–184.

* Comedy suffers from some of the same prejudices, as it likewise is a form often more idea driven than character driven. It is frequently as dependent as science fiction on "what if" scenarios ("What if two men had to dress in drag to escape gangsters?"), and of course, a joke itself is idea driven: You have to *get the joke* before it can make you laugh.

be for your story. This character development will only serve to draw the audience away from what it really came to see: how the *idea* plays out. You don't want your characters to function only as irritating distractions in any story. In science fiction, therefore, character must be invented and developed so that it brings out and supports the story's *idea*. As long as you pull that off, then you can then take character as far as you want it to go. There are, of course, subgenres of science fiction in which the sci-fi elements are used only for their trappings (as is the case with most so-called "space operas"), and in such cases a more traditional approach to character may actually be appropriate.

———

HIS PROTESTATIONS NOTWITHSTANDING, Aristotle does understand that character is demonstrated by *action*. Through their actions, we "determine what kinds of men are being presented." For Aristotle, the purpose of drama is to show how men become happy or miserable as a result of their actions. And so Aristotle's prescription for characterization is simply this: *Character is indicated by ACTIONS that demonstrate a person's CHOICE — what things the character chooses or rejects, for good or for evil.*

For Howard and Mabley, on the other hand, "The essence of characterization is the revelation of the inner life of the character." The key word here is *revelation*, or *revealing*. Novels have the luxury of explaining a character's inner life directly to the reader, but in a movie, TV show, or play, inner life doesn't even exist unless it's revealed in some external way. How does the writer achieve this? By deploying *obstacles*. In overcoming obstacles, a character's inner life is laid bare. It is possible, of course, for the character to talk about their inner life, but characterization is incomplete without showing that inner life acted out. Words are fine and dandy, but when the chips are down, we want to see what your character *does*.

Howard and Mabley's operational rule for characterization is, happily for our study, a structural one: *During the second act, intense pressure is put on the character to change* (otherwise stated as: "Will the main character stand up for him/herself?"), *and that change is manifested in the third act.*

Thus, if we stir Aristotle into Howard and Mabley, the result is the following recipe for character development:

(1) *Obstacles* provide the opportunity for a character to *make choices* through which the inner life of the character is revealed.

(2) In Act One, the character enters into conflict; Act Two puts *pressure* on the character to change; Act Three *changes* the character.

EXERCISES: DYNAMIC CHARACTER

1. Provide examples from three favorite films of a choice made by a character to overcome an obstacle, and what that choice reveals about the character's inner life.

Film _____

Character _____

Choice _____

Revelation of Inner Life _____

_____

Film _____

Character _____

Choice _____

Revelation of Inner Life _____

_____

Film _____

Character _____

Choice _____

Revelation of Inner Life _____

_____

2. Choose one of the characters selected above. Outline the pressures placed on him/her to change in Act Two of the screenplay, and detail the changes that are manifested in the character by the end of Act Three.

Film _____

Character _____

Act Two Pressures _____

_____

_____

Act Three Changes _____

_____

_____

Chapter Seven

STRUCTURAL ANALYSES,
or Don't Take My Word For It...

*The movie, by sheer speeding up of the mechanical, carried
us from the world of sequence and connections into the
world of creative configurations and structure.*

— Marshall McLuhan

To SUBJECT MY SYSTEM TO THE TORTURE TEST,
I will now perform structural analyses of twelve well-known
movies and plays. My purpose will be to examine these familiar
works through the spyglass of my "dynamic structure" concept,
and to see if I can superimpose my three-acts-with-a-conflict
template onto them without doing them too much violence.

I've picked several films and plays that illustrate the three-
act story structure that has always proven most satisfying to an
audience, along with a couple of atypically structured pieces
that work on their own terms and a few structurally flawed
specimens of the storyteller's art. Of these misshapen stories,
only one truly works as a story and a movie; it's one of those
exceptions that transcends the form, a dazzling display of sheer
inspiration that breaks the rules and gets away with it.

Before we get started, here is a thumbnail guide to analyzing
a screenplay using my system. This, with variations from film to
film, will be the basic template for the structural analyses in this
chapter. You will find that if you can provide solid answers to all
of these questions in the course of your analysis of any screenplay,
that screenplay is almost definitely structurally sound, and the
resultant film, while not necessarily any good, will at least "work"
as an example of three-act storytelling (as with my dynamic-structural rewrite of the doomed *Phobia* recounted in Chapter One).

TO ANALYZE A SCREENPLAY:

Take a look at the screenplay's structure. Are there three acts? If so, where do the first, second, and third acts break?

Who are the *antagonists*? (main character and his enemy)

What is the *issue of contention* between them?

What is the *conflict*?

When is the conflict defined, and in what manner? (Repeat this rule for any additional subconflicts that may be worked into the story).

What is The Point of No Return, if any? (What makes it a Point of No Return?)

How is/are the conflict/s resolved?

TO ANALYZE A CHARACTER:

What does the hero *want*? Are there *obstacles* in his path? Do they force him to make *choices*?

In *overcoming* those obstacles, is his *inner life revealed*?

Does he *enter into conflict* in Act One?

Is he *pressured to change* in Act Two?

Does he *change* in Act Three?

CASABLANCA
(1942; 103 min.)

Screenplay by
Julius J. Epstein, Philip G. Epstein,
and Howard Koch
Based on the play *Everybody Comes to Rick's*
by Murray Burnett and Joan Alison

MANY PEOPLE CONSIDER *CASABLANCA* the quint-essential Hollywood studio-system film, and its Academy Award–winning screenplay is widely regarded as a model of perfect Hollywood storytelling form... a fact all the more amazing when you consider the tangled circumstances under which that screenplay was created.

Jack Warner had bought this unproduced play called *Everybody Comes to Rick's*, which was not only timely, dealing as it does with European war refugees in North Africa, but also had the potential to be a great vehicle for one of his studio's stable of male stars. But the script needed a rewrite, a project he assigned to the prolific Epstein brothers.

Working under pressure of time, the Epsteins cranked out sixty-three pages of script before being called away on another assignment. With shooting to begin in six weeks, a junior member of the Warners' writing pool, Howard Koch, was assigned to the script. Koch wanted to get more political intrigue into the piece. For him, the romantic subplot was less important than the film's comments about the new world war against European fascism.

Koch turned in the first half of his draft four days before the commencement of shooting, but producer Hal Wallis and director Michael Curtiz were now unsatisfied with the script's handling of the romance, and thus they started filming with the picture's ending still up in the air.

A revised script (by who is not clear) appeared at the end of the first week of shooting, but in this draft the love triangle still remained unresolved. By this point, the actors were beginning to fret. Ingrid Bergman (Ilsa), in particular, wanted to know the ending so she would know how to play scenes with both Rick and Victor. Which man did she love more? Curtiz's advice to her? "Just play it in between." So Bergman's onscreen ambivalence in *Casablanca* is genuine, because she had no idea which man Ilsa would end up with. When Bergman (as Ilsa) says, "I don't know the finish [to our story] yet," and Humphrey Bogart (as Rick) replies, "Go on and tell it, maybe one'll come to you as you go along," they're stating a double truth, describing the situation both in front of and behind the cameras.

Nobody involved with the production of *Casablanca* seems to remember exactly who finally came up with the ending. The (unattributed) pages for the final scene were not delivered until the night before the scene was shot, and that great closing line — "Louis, I think this is the beginning of a beautiful friendship" — wasn't even thought up until after the film was edited! The producers came up with it while screening the final cut, and the line was subsequently recorded and dubbed over a shot of Rick's back as he walks away with Renault.

What's astonishing is how well these various convoluted efforts actually slot together. You would never guess that this screenplay was not the product of an elegantly unified vision from the very first page.

Analysis: Characters and Situation

Who are the characters? Though *Casablanca* has a large cast of characters, the principal focus is on three people: Rick Blaine, a cynical American nightclub owner in World War II–era North Africa; Ilsa Lund, the woman who loved and left Rick years ago; and Victor Laszlo, freedom fighter and Ilsa's husband.

What are the conflicts? Like a lot of stories with large casts, *Casablanca* has many conflicts. Some are crucial to the story, like Major Strasser's determination to keep Victor from escaping from Casablanca. Some are peripheral, like Rick's good-natured business rivalry with Signor Ferrari. Some are fleeting, like the narrowly averted fight between French and German soldiers in Rick's club. And, of course, all of these small conflicts play out against the large-scale conflict of World War II. Really, though, three main conflicts drive the narrative of *Casablanca*.

> Conflict #1: US VERSUS THEM. The war with the Nazis looms over every frame of this film. When Rick gives his band the nod to play "La Marseillaise," prompting a sing-along, led by Victor, that drowns out a crowd of Strasser's Nazis singing "Wacht am Rhein," the moment epitomizes

the conflict that underscores the entire film: *the issue of whether fascism or democracy will win the war.*

Conflict #2: THE LOVE TRIANGLE. Those who regard *Casablanca* as mainly a romance will no doubt feel that the film's primary conflict is the love triangle among Rick, Ilsa, and Victor. Ilsa finds herself torn between one man she loves with her heart, and another she worships for his courage and conviction. Issue of contention: *Who gets Ilsa?*

Conflict #3: A MAN DIVIDED. Still, for all its power, the romantic triangle is not what ultimately drives *Casablanca*. The most important conflict in the film is an internal one, within the character of Rick. The film's main conflict can thus be stated: *Will Rick regain his idealism, or remain a cynic and let the world fall to pieces around him?* The issue here is Rick's *character*, his *integrity*.

When are the conflicts defined, and in what manner?

Conflict #1: The war with the Nazis is present from the beginning of the film, a given. Victor and Strasser, the film's most extreme representatives of the war's opposing sides, first meet at Rick's, and frostily size each other up, about twenty-eight minutes into the film (27% of *Casablanca's* total running time).

Conflict #2: Rick and Ilsa come face to face in the film for the first time when she walks into his club with Victor, her husband. Their scorching glances tell us there's history here: Something has passed between these two. This moment occurs at the thirty-three-minute mark, just one third of the way into the film. End of the first act.

Conflict #3: Nineteen minutes into the film (18% of the running time), Renault says probingly, "Ricky, I suspect that under that cynical shell, you're at heart a sentimentalist." This line tells us that Rick is a better man than he lets on. So when's he going to start acting better? This question defines Rick's inner conflict.

Throughout the film, Rick is peppered with questions about his loyalties. By bringing him the letters of transit eleven minutes into the picture (11%), the smuggler Ugarte puts him on the spot: What will he do with these universal objects of desire? This question, an "outer" conflict that helps to dramatize Rick's inner conflict, will not be answered until the end of the film.

What is The Point of No Return? Seventy-four minutes into the film (72%), Renault shuts down Rick's club under orders from Major Strasser. Conflict #1 is closing in on Rick; he can't stay neutral much longer.

Shortly after this scene, Ilsa comes to Rick's apartment and demands at gunpoint that he turn over the letters of transit; she needs them to help her and Victor escape Casablanca and the Nazis. Still, she can't bring herself to pull the trigger on the man she used to love, even when he exhorts her to, at perhaps the lowest moment he reaches in his struggle with Conflict #3 ("Go ahead and shoot. You'd be doing me a favor"). Then, as Rick and Ilsa hold each other, eighty-five minutes into the film (83%), their Point of No Return arrives, and Rick finally makes a statement of commitment:

ILSA: You will have to think for both of us... for all of us.
RICK: All right. I will.

The die is now cast. Rick will expose himself to potential arrest and execution to help Ilsa escape with Victor. (Of course, one of the great things about this screenplay is that at this point, the viewer doesn't know Rick's going to let Ilsa go; we only know that he's at last committed himself to taking some sort of stand. In a way, this decision demonstrates dramatic irony in reverse, as the protagonist knows something we don't, thus priming us for exciting revelations later in the film.) Conflicts #2 and #3 have both reached their turning points. *The conflicts are converging.*

It's quite difficult to make multiple conflicts fuse as one with this kind of economy. It's a beautiful job of writing. Of course, the writers do have those all-purpose letters of transit to whip out every time they need to explain the unexplainable. That's the value of a good MacGuffin*... and remember, Victor himself is somewhat of a MacGuffin, too.

How are the conflicts resolved? At the airstrip, Rick springs his big surprise by trading the letters of transit for two tickets to Lisbon "for Mr. and Mrs. Victor Laszlo." As he sends Ilsa away, he admits that there's more to life than himself, that when the world is at war, "The problems of three little people don't amount to a hill of beans." This moment, ninety-seven minutes into the film (94%), resolves Conflicts #2 and #3.

And, even though Major Strasser ultimately eats a bullet from Rick, Conflict #1, of course, would remain unresolved until after the production wrapped.

EXERCISE: *CASABLANCA*
In *Casablanca*, Ilsa tells Rick that he "will have to think for both of us... for all of us," thus leaving him to make the decisions that resolve Conflicts #2 and #3. What if Rick had left it up to Ilsa to choose between himself and Victor on her own? Based on what has come before this moment in *Casablanca*, describe how Act Three might have played out if Ilsa had been left to make the decision between the two men. Would Conflicts #2 and #3 have resolved in the same way? How would the film's resolution be different?

_____

_____

_____

_____

_____

*Defined as "an object of universal desire that drives a story," the term is usually attributed to Hitchcock.

CITIZEN KANE
(1941, 119 min.)

Screenplay by Herman J. Mankiewicz
and Orson Welles

OFTEN CALLED, WITH SOME JUSTICE, "The greatest movie ever made," *Citizen Kane* is a cornucopia of wonderful writing. The dialogue is a pageant of delightful and profound words that are a consistent pleasure to listen to. None of that comes from structure, and it, as much as anything, helped Mankiewicz and Welles win a Best Original Screenplay Oscar (which was, famously, the only Oscar the film received). The script for *Citizen Kane* is, if anything, even better than the film. It would be worth your while to chase down a copy, for the illuminating experience of reading it, not to mention the sheer pleasure of the thing.

At first blush, *Citizen Kane* would appear to be quite structurally complex, what with its heavy usage of flashbacks and shifting narrative points of view, but upon closer examination, the structure reveals itself to be quite clear and easy to track.

Analysis: Characters and Situation

Who are the characters? Early twentieth-century media magnate Charles Foster Kane, and "Everyone who ever worked for him, who ever loved him, who ever hated his guts."

What are the conflicts? This film, like *Casablanca*, features multiple conflicts among characters. Kane's boyhood guardian, Thatcher, bristles at the young Kane's liberal politics; Gettys and Kane compete against one another in a gubernatorial election; Susan and Kane clash over his desire to make her an opera star, and so on. These conflicts add color to the drama, but none of them ultimately drives the story. This function is largely served here by two primarily conflicts.

Conflict #1: KANE VERSUS THE WORLD. Throughout his life (and thus the film), Kane moves from conflict to conflict, with other newspapers, with Gettys, with the treacherous waters of public opinion. He needs his battles, feeds off them, nurtures himself with his victories. But the world is always there, indomitable, ready with a fresh windmill for Kane to tilt at. The "issue": *Will Kane bring the world to heel?*

Conflict #2: KANE VERSUS HIMSELF. The film's main conflict, of course, is fought out in Kane's interior spaces. Here is a man who desperately wants love, but who learned as a boy the wounding lesson that money was more powerful than love, and who came of age in circumstances where the accumulation of power through wealth outweighed any other human consideration. Throughout the film, these two sides of Kane — the romantic idealist and the greedy tyrant — drive the narrative as they battle for control of Kane's life. The "issue": *Kane's principles and where they will guide him.*

When are the conflicts defined, and in what manner?

Conflict #1: The conflict between Kane and the world at large could scarcely be more literal; the young newspaper mogul boasts of starting a war to improve his paper's circulation,* and later using the paper's power to prevent a different conflict. His various disputes with the planet are sketched out even earlier than this undertaking, in the "News on the March" newsreel reporting Kane's death, which occurs in the film's very first sequence. In the newsreel's nine minutes, Kane is broadly and variously condemned as the personification of virtually every social evil on the political

---

*In one of many moments of narrative and dialogue that draw inspiration from the life of *Kane's* unspoken source subject, media baron William Randolph Hearst, Kane tells one of his reporters, "You provide the prose poems; I'll provide the war." This is a direct paraphrase of a telegram Hearst sent to one of his own journalists on the eve of the Spanish-American War, a conflict believed to have been at least partially instigated by Spanish-excoriating articles in Hearst's newspapers.

spectrum; at one point, he is even shown sharing a balcony with Hitler.

Conflict #2: Twenty-six minutes into the film (22% of the running time), Kane, now a young man who has already begun making noise as the crusading editor-in-chief of the *New York Inquirer*, comes right out and describes himself, in a confrontation with Thatcher (a money-grubbing plutocrat with no Kane-like duality or inner doubt), as two people:

As Charles Foster Kane, who owns 82,364 shares of Public Transit, Preferred... you see, I do have a general idea of my holdings... I sympathize with you. Charles Foster Kane is a scoundrel. His paper should be run out of town. A committee should be formed to boycott him. You may, if you can form such a committee, put me down for a contribution of one thousand dollars. On the other hand, I am the publisher of the *Inquirer*. As such, it is my duty, and I'll let you in on a little secret – it's also my pleasure – to see to it that decent, hard-working people in this community aren't robbed blind by a pack of money-mad pirates, just because they haven't anybody to look after their interests.

The timing of this duality-defining speech demarcates it as the first-act curtain, setting the stage for Idealist Kane versus Tyrant Kane.

What is The Point of No Return? Early on in Kane's struggle with himself, the idealist seems to have the upper hand. He is blessed with a politically advantageous marriage, his newspapers guide and shape public opinion worldwide, and he seems to be living in a way consistent with the rose-colored "Declaration of Principles" that he printed in the first edition of the *Inquirer*, published under his name. Even an affair with Susan Alexander, an aspiring singer he puts up in a private "love nest," does little to stall his rise to the top, and when he makes a run for the governor's office, it seems that almost nothing can stop him.

Kane's Waterloo is the exposure of his affair with Susan Alexander by his electoral opponent, Boss Jim Gettys.* Until this point, the two halves of Kane's personality have coexisted in a rough harmony. But when his adultery is bared to the world, he is forced to decide what he wants to be, and his dreams are dashed when his choice to stand by Susan costs him the election. From this collapse, seventy minutes into the film (60%), there is no going back. The idealistic side of Kane goes into remission, and the tyrant emerges full-blown.

How are the conflicts resolved? As Kane's former friend Jedediah Leland tells it, "He [Kane] was disappointed in the world, so he built one of his own." Xanadu, Kane's seaside mansion, makes its grim debut ninety-eight minutes into the film (82%). It's a huge tomb built for two, Kane and Susan, a place for Kane to withdraw from the world with which he had so adeptly sparred during his journalistic career. Kane forfeits the fight. But the world is still there, still passing judgment on Kane and all others. Conflict #1 is resolved. The world has won.

At first, it might seem that Conflict #2 is resolved when Kane, amid the rubble of Susan's opera career (that he forced her into against her will), tears up the original copy of his "Declaration of Principles." It would be hard to imagine a more definitive withdrawal from one's idealism than that: Kane has taken the high standards of his younger days and literally torn them to pieces. He presides over Xanadu like a tyrant, his spiritual domination of Susan eventually devolving into physical violence. The further inward Kane turns, the further he likewise seems from his idealistic self.

But then, 106 minutes into the film (89%), Susan finally walks out on Kane. (Welles the director illustrates Kane's terrifying

---

*Another individual who is able to get the best of Kane because he, unlike Kane, is not burdened with inner conflict; Gettys fully admits, "I am not a gentleman. I don't even know what a gentleman is."

isolation in the famous compound mirror shot: Kane alone, but multiplied into infinity). At this moment, the idealist re-emerges, and Kane, with nothing left but his memories, reaches out for "Rosebud," the spiritual embodiment of his lost childhood innocence. But the damage has been done. The game is over. Kane dies without ever finding "Rosebud."

⸻

ONE OF THE MANY THINGS that made *Citizen Kane* so revolutionary upon its initial release was that it was told almost entirely in flashback, something that had never been done in Hollywood before. Though Thompson's quest to discover the meaning of Kane's last word exists essentially to frame the film's main story, it nevertheless has its own Howard-and-Mabley-style dramatic structure, with a conflict, culmination, and resolution (see p. 44 of the present book).

In this subplot, the conflict is defined fourteen minutes into the film (12% of the running time), when Thompson is assigned to find "Rosebud, dead or alive." The culmination is reached at the 107-minute mark (90%), when Thompson goes to Xanadu, the heart of Kane's world, to interview the insinuating butler who "knows where all the bodies are buried." Then, at 112 minutes (94%), Thompson gives up his search, conceding that "Rosebud" is probably just "a piece in a jigsaw puzzle. A missing piece." And just for the three of you out there who don't already know it, I'll leave the meaning of "Rosebud" a secret.

EXERCISE: *CITIZEN KANE*
Citizen Kane is legendary for its groundbreaking nonlinear structure. How would the film's structure be altered if the story had been told in an entirely linear fashion? Looking at *Citizen Kane*, and omitting no scenes from the screenplay, outline the sequence of events if the story had been told linearly. What would the first- and second-act breaks be? Would

this decision fundamentally alter the film's conflicts and their resolution? Would the Thompson subplot still possess its own separate structure?

First-Act Break _____

_____

Second-Act Break _____

_____

Third-Act Resolution _____

_____

Structure of Thompson Subplot (If It Still Exists) _____

_____

_____

_____

_____

_____

_____

CROUCHING TIGER, HIDDEN DRAGON
(2000, 120 min.)

Screenplay by Hui-Ling Wang, James Schamus,
and Kuo Jung Tsai
Based on the novel by Du Lu Wang

CROUCHING TIGER, HIDDEN DRAGON is the highest grossing foreign language film ever released in the United States,* the only one to top $100 million at the U.S. box office. Much of this success was attributed at the time to its high-flying martial arts action; the film's fight scenes granted its combatants gravity-defying powers that solidified the "wire fu" trend in

---

* Or at least the highest-grossing actually produced by a foreign nation. The U.S.'s highest-grossing film entirely in a foreign language? *The Passion of the Christ*, at a little over $370 million.

American action movies. But a lot of the film's success can also be credited to a solid three-act structure that would be very familiar and comfortable to American viewers. The film's director, the Taiwanese Ang Lee, studied film production at NYU, and one of *Crouching Tiger's* writers, Lee's longtime collaborator James Schamus, is a U.S. native. Lee and Schamus, along with cowriters, Hui-Ling Wang and Kuo Jung Tsai, were thus able to bring a Western storytelling sensibility to Eastern material, winning them unprecedented box office success (not to mention an Academy Award for Best Foreign Language Film).

Analysis: Characters and Situation

Who are the characters? Five principal characters drive the action in *Crouching Tiger*: Longtime warrior comrades Li Mu Bai and Shu Lien; Lo, a desert warlord known as "Dark Cloud"; Jen Yu, a governor's daughter and secret martial arts master; and "Jade Fox," a legendary female criminal who killed Li Mu Bai's master and who, under disguise as a maid, has taught Jen martial arts from a forbidden book stolen from the monastery where Li Mu Bai learned his skills.

What are the conflicts? Two principal conflicts drive the story in *Crouching Tiger* — one thematic, one very much action oriented.

> Conflict #1: TRADITION VERSUS DESIRE. All of *Crouching Tiger's* main characters are caught up in a struggle between the time-tested traditions of their culture and their own unspoken desires, which run counter to their obedience to those traditions.
>
> Li Mu Bai and Shu Lien are warriors, sworn to monkish lives devoted to meditation and honing their fighter's craft. But this devotion conflicts with their love for one another, a love which they, over a decade-plus of fighting together, have never expressed to one another. (The situation is complicated by the fact that Shu Lien is the former love of Li

Mu Bai's best friend, who died on the battlefield and who, with his dying breath, made Li promise to look after Shu.)

Jen is also in conflict with society's expectations. She's the daughter of a powerful governor and on the verge of an arranged marriage to a man she's never met. But she craves adventure, romance, the kind of life she's read about in fantastical books about warriors like Li and Shu. She lives a secret double life as a warrior thief with great but undisciplined combat skills.

Jade Fox plays out an almost tragic variation of Jen's conflict. She was a woman who craved nothing more than the life of a warrior but was rejected from Wudan Monastery's legendary combat school.* She fought back by stealing a book of Wudan's fighting secrets (killing Li's master in the process) and secretly training both herself and Jen to fight. But her skills are half formed; as a servant, she cannot read, so she was only able to study the book's pictures, and she is deeply betrayed when she discovers that Jen (who can read) has surpassed her as a fighter.

Lo has chosen the easiest path in his struggle with tradition versus desire. He lives entirely outside society, as a desert warrior chieftain, sustaining himself by attacking travelers and looting their wares. But his life is complicated when he attacks the caravan of Jen's family, stealing her ivory hair comb. She chases him to get it back, becomes his captive, and eventually succumbs to the charms and romance of his lifestyle, falling in love with him. But how is a governor's daughter supposed to share her life with a fugitive warrior prince?

All of these conflicts are brought to the fore of the characters' lives by....

---

* Jade Fox says she was rejected because of her gender, but this excuse doesn't track, considering that Shu Lien, who was trained at Wudan, is a woman also. Perhaps Jade Fox was not born into the warrior class from which Shu Lien obviously hails, making her rejection more a question of class than of gender. Either way, Jade Fox sees it as a purely patriarchal rejection, and she chooses to ignore the contradiction.

Conflict #2: THE SWORD. A classic MacGuffin, the Green Destiny sword once belonged to Li's master and was passed down to Li at his master's death. At the beginning of the film, Li, weary of the warrior's life, has given the sword to Shu Lien to present as a gift to their mutual friend Sir Te. This sword will change hands several times through the course of the film, and it comes to represent different things to the characters who pursue it. Li and Shu see it as a reminder of the wages of a life lived in combat, whereas to Jen and Jade Fox, it represents the lives of adventure and excitement that society had tried to deny them.

When are the conflicts defined, and in what manner? The film begins with Shu Lien arriving at Sir Te's house with the Green Destiny sword. The same day, the governor and his family, including Jen, arrive to spend the night as they prepare for Jen's impending wedding. That night, a masked warrior (later revealed to be Jen) steals the sword and escapes after a martial arts battle with Shu Lien. This event occurs twenty-one minutes into the film (18% of the running time), ending Act One and defining Conflict #2: *Who will end up with the sword?*

As Conflict #2 plays out, the various permutations of Conflict #1 begin to reveal themselves. We've already seen in Act One that Li and Shu have a bond closer than friendship. But we also know that Li swore an oath to his dead friend, Shu's former lover, an oath that consummating his own feelings for her would betray.

Act Two gives us signs that Jen is unhappy with her life as a governor's daughter. She seems unenthusiastic about her wedding, and she's drawn to Shu's life as a roaming warrior, free and independent (at least that's how she sees it). Clues to her identity as a covert warrior are planted throughout the first half of Act Two, notably in a moment when Shu, suspicious of Jen, intentionally knocks a porcelain serving dish off a table. Jen, with lightning-fast reflexes, catches it and replaces it so fast that the saucer underneath doesn't even slip loose.

Conflict #2 takes a turn forty-five minutes into the film (38%) when Li Mu Bai fights the masked Jen and reclaims Green Destiny. Shortly after this event, forty-seven minutes in (39%), Jen is revealed as the masked warrior, and we learn the story of her secret training by her maid, who is actually the wanted murderer known as Jade Fox. The former criminal speaks of her thwarted desire to be a great warrior, and how social strictures forced her to rebel by stealing the Wudan combat book. Jen and Jade Fox are paired as fellow rebels against the system, though Jen's rebellion is presented in a more innocent, romantic spirit, whereas Jade Fox's has already hardened into bitterness and overtly insurrectionist feelings.

Then, a new wrinkle arrives in the form of Lo, who comes to Jen fifty-three minutes into the film (44%), kicking off a nearly twenty-minute-long flashback sequence that fills in Jen's backstory. We learn that her craving for adventure was stirred by her desert idyll with Lo, and that he still loves her and wants her to abandon her planned marriage and be with him. When she is unwilling to take that risk (mostly out of fear for Lo's safety), Lo commits the most overt assault on tradition in the entire film when, seventy-four minutes in (62%), he attacks Jen's wedding parade and beseeches her to come away with him. She refuses, but later that night, she runs away... and takes Green Destiny with her. Conflict #2 re-ignites, seventy-six minutes into the film (63%).

What is The Point of No Return? After talking to Lo and sending him away to Wudan Monastery to wait for them, Li and Shu track down Jen. The two women have a major battle ninety minutes into the film (75%), the tradition-bound warrior versus her rebellious mirror image. The battle is later joined by Li Mu Bai, who challenges Jen to place the sword above her own safety, throwing it off the side of a cliff. Jen jumps to retrieve it, but is snatched before she can hit the water below by Jade Fox, who carries her away, along with the sword. It's ninety-nine minutes into the film, 83% of the running time. Jade Fox now has both

Jen and the sword. Li Mu Bai and Shu Lien will have to battle the woman who killed Li's master if they hope to reclaim the sword... and rescue Jen from the sad life Jade Fox chose when she proved herself willing to kill for her desires. Only one option remains for these characters: take-no-prisoners, to-the-death combat. Conflicts #1 and #2 dovetail nicely as we reach The Point of No Return.

How are the conflicts resolved? Li and Shu track Jade Fox to her lair in a watery cave. Li battles Jade Fox, who, before she is killed, strikes Li with a poison dart (104 minutes in; 87%). Jen runs off to find ingredients for an antidote, but Li dies before she can return. Before he dies, Li tells Shu that he has always loved her and expires in her arms. One hundred and nine minutes in (91%), Conflict #1 resolves for Li and Shu, tragically, as their bond to the warrior tradition ultimately wins out over their love for one another.

Conflict #2 is resolved 112 minutes into the film (93%) as Shu returns the sword to Sir Te. She sends Jen to Wudan Monastery to meet with Lo, and Jen reminds him of a myth they spoke of in the desert, of a young man who made a wish and took a leap of faith from a mountain. Lo wishes that he and Jen were back in the desert together, and Jen casts her lot with desire over tradition as she herself leaps from Wudan Mountain (114 minutes in, 95%). Does she survive? Is Lo's wish granted? The film cuts to black before we find out... but considering the way we've been watching these characters flying around for two hours, my money's on things working out okay.

EXERCISES: *CROUCHING TIGER, HIDDEN DRAGON*
1. One of the secrets of *Crouching Tiger, Hidden Dragon's* unprecedented success with American audiences is its screenplay's adherence to "Western" three-act screenwriting structure. Are there any noteworthy ways in which the film

deviates from standard structure and seems to suggest a more "Eastern" manner of storytelling?

_____

_____

_____

_____

2. Can you name a foreign film in which the screenplay structure seems to adhere to a model more familiar in its country of origin? Does the film have three acts? If so, where do the act breaks occur? If it has a different number of acts, how many does it possess and where do the act breaks happen?

_____

_____

_____

_____

A DOLL'S HOUSE
(1879; 106 pages in the Faber and Faber edition)

Play written by Henrik Ibsen

BACK AT THE BEGINNING OF CHAPTER Three, I mentioned the six authorities on dramatic structure, and said that Ibsen was the only one who had not written his own book of structural concepts and rules. Even though he never put his method down on paper, modern dramatic structure begins with Ibsen, and *A Doll's House* is the play that elevated the Norwegian playwright to the ranks of the world's premiere dramatic writers.

My favorite historian, Paul Johnson, says, "He not only invented modern drama, but wrote a succession of plays which still form a substantial part of its entire repertoire... he not only revolutionized his art but changed the social thinking of his generation and the one that came after...."[16]

Prior to Ibsen, most plays were published in book form before being performed, if they ever saw the stage at all. Written in poetry, they were usually more suitable for reading than acting. It was Ibsen who "reached the systematic conclusion that such plays would have infinitely more impact if presented on stage than read in the study. That led him to renounce poetry and embrace prose, and with it a new kind of theatrical realism... each work is fundamentally different, usually a new step into the unknown... Ibsen asked disturbing questions about the power of money, the oppression of women, even the taboo subject of sexual disease. He placed fundamental political and social issues literally at the center of the stage, in simple, everyday language in settings all could recognize... They were the first modern plays.[17]"

A Doll's House "is widely considered a landmark in the development of what soon became a highly prevalent genre of theater – *realism*, which strives to portray life accurately and shuns idealized visions of it. In *A Doll's House*, Ibsen employs the themes and structures of classical tragedy while writing in prose about everyday, unexceptional people. Ibsen followed *A Doll's House* with two plays written in an innovative, realistic mode: *Ghosts*, in 1881, and *An Enemy of the People*, in 1882. Both were successes."[18]

A Doll's House does fit my structural system, but only just. The Point of No Return comes extremely late in this play. I wouldn't change it, though. This work offers a case where inspiration trumps rules (more on this in Chapter Thirteen), and it's worth remembering that Ibsen was plowing virgin soil. In such circumstances, some ragged rows are to be expected.

---

[16] Paul Johnson, *Intellectuals: From Marx and Tolstoy to Sartre and Chomsky* (New York: HarperCollins, 1988), 82.

[17] Ibid, 85–86.

[18] Sparknotes: *A Doll's House* (New York: Barnes & Noble, 2002), 1-2.

Analysis: Characters and Situation

Who are the characters? An upper-middle-class Danish house-wife named Nora Helmer, her full-of-himself husband, Torvald, and their friends and business associates, most notably a weaselly bank clerk named Krogstad.

What are the conflicts?

Conflict #1: NORA VERSUS KROGSTAD. The engine that drives the action here is a convoluted blackmail scheme. Nora once committed a wrongdoing for love: She faked her dead father's signature on a promissory note, using the money for a trip abroad that saved her husband's life. Krogstad also once committed forgery to save the life of the person he loved, but he was caught and publicly disgraced. Meanwhile, his wife died, leaving him to raise their children alone.

Krogstad unearths Nora's crime, and the realization that her forgery saved a socially advantageous marriage, while the same offense threw him into poverty, and disrepute stirs him to extortion. He threatens to expose Nora's past misdeed, in the rather thin hope that she will persuade her husband to step down from his job and convince his bank to hire Krogstad as a replacement. Everything that follows, Kristine's reunion with Krogstad, Torvald's denunciation of Nora, and Nora's awakening and abandonment of her family, stems from Krogstad's desperate threat.

Conflict #2: NORA VERSUS TORVALD (READ: WOMAN VERSUS MAN). Those who view *A Doll's House* as a primarily political work will see the play's main conflict within the society at large — specifically, the different standards to which society holds men and women. On Ibsen's stage, men have all the power and influence, while Nora is Torvald's "little singing bird," a "squirrel" forced to dance and do tricks for his money and affection.

Torvald wants his wife to believe that the issue that divides them is her bad character. In reality, the play's social context — the inequities accorded men and women — precipitates Krogstad's threat (after all, a man who commits the same crime as a woman is punished for it) and is therefore truly the play's main conflict. Issue of contention: *The battle of the sexes*.

When are the conflicts defined, and in what manner? *A Doll's House* is a three-act play, and Ibsen's first-act break, as it happens, corresponds to where the first-act break in my structural system would fall. Near the end of Ibsen's Act One (which ends on p. 41, 39% of the play's 106 pages), Krogstad approaches Nora with his demands. He reveals his knowledge of her forgery, and threatens to ruin both her and Torvald unless she helps him usurp her husband's bank job: "If I am hurled back into the gutter a second time, you will keep me company." Act One thus ends with Conflict #1 defined: Nora must find a way to keep Krogstad from exposing her transgression, which, in the world of the play, is a serious crime with the power to ruin lives if brought to light.

Conflict #2, at this point in the play, has not really been concretely defined as a conflict at all. The social disparity between men and women is already there in Torvald's master-and-pet relationship with his wife, but at the immediate moment, and for a long while yet, it is not presented as a point of contention between the characters.

What is The Point of No Return? Nora suffers through the play's second act and most of the third, agonizing over when Krogstad's axe will fall. Near the end of Act Two, Krogstad drops a letter in the Helmers' mailbox that exposes Nora's secret. Torvald doesn't read it, though, until nearly the end of Act Three (p. 92; 87%), and when he does, he blows his stack and says things to Nora that cannot be retracted. Unmoved by the fact that her forgery was committed to save his life, he rants on about his reputation, proclaiming that the marriage will have to be continued as a charade for appearance's sake, and that Nora, "criminal" that she is, "liar" and "hypocrite" with "no morals, no sense of duty," will be permitted no further contact with their children. In his petulant fury, he manages to so overstate the case (and makes a flaming asshole of himself generally) that he shatters the marriage beyond repair. Conflict #2, therefore, is introduced (at least as an overt theme of the play) and brought to its Point of No Return at almost the exact same moment, a difficult trick to make work, especially so late in the play.

How are the conflicts resolved? In a sudden reversal, near the end of Act Three, Krogstad meets with a minor character named Kristine, established earlier in the play as an old friend of Nora. It is revealed that she and Krogstad were once lovers, and she offers now to return to him and be his wife and mother to his children. This reunion solves Krogstad's problems (at least in his own mind), and in his joy, he sends Torvald another letter that lets Nora off the hook. Conflict #1 resolved... but Ibsen's just getting started.

When he reads Krogstad's new letter, Torvald exults: "I'm saved!" Nora is stunned to see that her husband cares only for his own salvation, and Torvald only makes things worse when he reverses his previous condemnations of her... and then praises himself for being so forgiving.

Nora is no longer under threat from Krogstad, but she now sees her own husband as a tyrant, imprisoning her within a narrow domestic box, making her a "doll-wife" and suppressing any expression of her true self. She undergoes a feminist awakening and leaves both Torvald and her children to go fulfill "my duties to myself" (p. 101; 95%). Conflict #2 is resolved for Nora, if not for society as a whole.

This character reversal is not only absolute, but it's also extremely abrupt; we are not prepared for it by anything that comes before in the play. Still, *A Doll's House* was one of the first plays to directly tackle the issue of feminism, and one suspects it is this politicized finale, rather than the unremarkable blackmail story, that has earned the play its reputation as a classic.

EXERCISE: *A DOLL'S HOUSE*
It is stated above that nothing in the first hundred pages of *A Doll's House* prepares the audience for the feminist awakening Nora undergoes at the end of Act Three. Do you agree with this statement? Can you find any examples of actions or dialogue in the first two and three-quarter acts of Ibsen's play that fore-shadow Nora's character reversal? Is the "man versus woman in society" conflict truly a driving force in the drama of *A Doll's House?*

_____

_____

_____

_____

_____

DRACULA
(1931, 75 min.)

Screenplay by Garrett Fort
Based on the novel by Bram Stoker
and the stage play by Hamilton Deane
and John L. Balderston*

LOOKING AT EFFECTIVELY STRUCTURED FILMS is only one half of the learning process. It is just as illuminating to study stories with serious structural problems. Knowing what

---

* The Internet Movie Database lists an additional five uncredited writers for *Dracula*: director Tod Browning; "contributing writers" Louis Bromfield and Louis Stevens; Dudley Murphy, credited with "additional dialogue"; and Max Cohen, credited with "titles." Not the 32 writers who allegedly wrote the *Flintstones* movie, but it'll do.

doesn't work, and why, can suddenly make it clear what you *should* do.

An otherwise good film may be structurally flawed, and it is rare, but not unheard of, to come across a well-regarded picture that is a structural shambles. The iconic Bela Lugosi–starring adaptation of *Dracula* is one of the all-time classic horror films, and Lugosi's performance as the blood-drinking undead aristocrat has become iconic. This magnificence appears despite a screenplay that, to put it politely, has some issues.

With so many people working on this script, you'd think they could have gotten it right, but not all pictures with screenplays by committee fall into place like *Casablanca*. (In all fairness, Stoker's rambling, largely epistolary novel is almost unadaptable; to date, no one has produced a fully satisfactory version. Probably the best structured was Murnau's silent *Nosferatu*, and that was achieved at the expense of eliminating Van Helsing!)

Analysis: Characters and Situation

Who are the characters? The hemophagic Carpathian Count Dracula and his unsuspecting human prey.

What are the conflicts? Any vampire film, *Dracula* included, trades on cosmic themes of good and evil, light and darkness. The "natural" qualities of humanity are cast in opposition to the powers of the vampire, who drinks living blood, transmogrifies into animals, and walks only by night. As the living dead, the vampire is an abomination of nature, an affront to God's divine plan. Therefore, the film inherently dramatizes a conflict between purity and contamination, one that has made the vampire genre a favorite of Freudian film critics who have interpreted various vampire pictures as everything from cautionary tales of sullied Victorian ladyhood to AIDS allegories.

Conflict #1: DRACULA VERSUS HUMANITY. *Dracula*, of course, is driven by an external conflict, the blood-drenched Count versus the world. The vampire desires to feed on the living; the forces of civilization array themselves against him. The issue is the *fate of humankind*, embodied by Mina and Van Helsing and the rest.

Conflict #2: MINA'S STRUGGLE. The film's internal conflict is manifested in the character of Mina. As Dracula feeds on her, she finds herself drawn to his darkness, but the human half of her soul resists the temptation to submit to the vampire's power. She is the film's central human embodiment of the light-versus-darkness motif. The issue is *the fate of Mina's soul*. (For what it's worth, poor enslaved Renfield also suffers an internal conflict that serves as a kind of "supporting conflict"; his compulsion to serve the Count is resisted by a longing to rescue Mina from his fate. The issue, then, is really *Mina's soul, and to a lesser extent, Renfield's*.)

When are the conflicts defined, and in what manner? From the start, Count Dracula is clearly dangerously evil. The peasants warn Renfield that the Count is an unnatural creature, and — in case there was any doubt — the first time we see him, he's emerging from a coffin. He can walk through spider webs without breaking them (an effect better stage managed in the justly famous Spanish-language version, which we'll discuss more in Chapter Twelve), he recoils from a crucifix, and he's all too interested in the blood that oozes from a cut on Renfield's finger.

Finally, when Renfield passes out at the sight of Dracula's undead brides, the Count seizes the opportunity to make a meal of him. We're eighteen minutes into the film (24% of the running time), and there's no doubt about it. Dracula is a monster, and he's on his way to the heart of civilization. End of Act One; Conflict #1 defined. So far, so good. And now it gets sticky.

Act Two: first sign of structural trouble. When they arrive in London, Dracula and Renfield are the only two characters we have gotten to know in this film. But Renfield, who is now a ranting, bug-eating lunatic, promptly gets thrown into an asylum, leaving Dracula, now the only character tethering us to this plot, free to roam the streets, searching for fresh victims.

He finds them at the theater, where he meets Dr. Seward, the director of the asylum that has incarcerated Renfield, along with his daughter, Mina, her friend Lucy, and Mina's fiancé, John Harker. These characters, never even mentioned in the first act, now take over as the film's protagonists, even though we've spent the whole first act with Renfield. It's almost like what screenwriter Joseph Stefano did with *Psycho*'s infamous "false first act" (more on this later in this chapter), where Marion's murder hands the story over to Norman Bates. But in that film, the plot's focus was at least transferred between two characters whose stories overlapped. Here, when Renfield is removed from the main action at the beginning of Act Two, the narrative focus is shunted over to completely unfamiliar characters. (In the original novel, it's John Harker, something of a nonentity in this film, who travels to Transylvania. Renfield, a former partner at the law firm where Harker works, is already institutionalized when the story begins, and Harker is sent to the Count's castle to finish business that Renfield's breakdown left him unable to complete. Something of that sort would have worked better,* as it would have given us an entry point into this new group of characters foisted on us unannounced in *Dracula's* second act.)

As the movie lurches into the meat of its second act, Dracula sets about his parasitic work, killing Lucy and turning her into a vampire who preys on children (something we hear about but never see, one of many ways this film betrays its stage origins). Then, the vampire sets his sights on Mina and starts paying her

---

* And, indeed, did in *Nosferatu*.

nightly visits, drawing her (and us) into Conflict #2. Still, the screenplay never bothers to make clear exactly what about Mina makes her so important to the Count. He hasn't even seen her picture back at his castle, as he does in other film versions. His choice to torment this particular girl seems utterly random, so there's really no reason why Mina stands at the center of this *Dracula*. He could be feeding on literally any woman in London.

What is The Point of No Return? When things get really dark, Van Helsing, an old friend of Dr. Seward, comes to London. Van Helsing knows all about vampires, and at forty-three minutes (58%), he "outs" Dracula with a crucifix and a mirror. This confrontation *should* have been The Point of No Return, at least for Conflict #1, as it primes us to expect a final titanic battle between the vampire and the scientist. We think we know where the third act is going, but remember: The second act didn't develop as we reasonably expected. This confrontation between Dracula and Van Helsing is really a false Point of No Return, something we don't usually see in a film unless it's done to startle us with a fleeting "the-monster's-not-really-dead" kind of moment. But that's not what happens here. It's just gumming up the story.

The *real* Point of No Return takes place at the sixty-eight-minute mark (91%), when Dracula kidnaps Mina and spirits her off to Carfax Abbey. The gauntlet is down, and both conflicts have simultaneously reached their Points of No Return, as the innocent woman, and thus all of civilization, is in mortal peril. Van Helsing and Harker give chase. *Now, finally*, we think: *The big payoff.*

Silly us.

How are the conflicts resolved? Van Helsing and Harker arrive at the abbey, where Dracula kills off Renfield, who has escaped and followed Dracula there (and who Van Helsing and Harker have followed to find the Count). They pursue the vampire into the lair and, finally, the doctor and the vampire square off! Right? Wrong. When they get inside the chamber, they find

Dracula already asleep in his coffin. So Van Helsing stakes him (off-screen, no less), and we hear the vampire's dying groans. That's it. No big battle to the death between good, embodied by Van Helsing, and evil, "personified" by Dracula. I understand that an early Hollywood talkie couldn't very well shower the audience with gore at the end, but we deserve a little better than the horror-film equivalent of a champion prizefighter taking a dive. Then, for the cherry on this anticlimactic sundae, Mina, who's now snapped out of her trance, informs Harker that it wasn't Van Helsing's stake that did Dracula in after all, but the rising sun. Conflicts #1 and #2 are thus resolved, simultaneously, by a stray beam of sunlight. To be fair, the earlier praised *Nosferatu* likewise ends with the vampire getting cooked alive by the sun... but that film had no Van Helsing to take on the Count. Here, it just feels like we're not getting what we paid to see.

Van Helsing now tells John and Mina to go, and we end the film with a stirring shot of the young lovers walking up the abbey steps into the sunlight that saved them. This rushed finale has a disconcerting abruptness (it plays much faster than I've described it here), in part because this conclusion is not at all what the novel does. This scene actually takes place in the novel's late middle, and the novel follows it with a thrilling chase back to the vampire's Transylvanian castle, where they dispatch him with satisfying thoroughness.* None of that happens here.

Still, this messy script proves, as if it needed to be proved at this point, that telling a perfect story is in no way required to make a hit, as long as you deliver what the audience is looking for, which in this case was some old-school scares... not to mention one of the most legendary performances of all time.

---

*This chase does occur in Francis Ford Coppola's 1992 adaptation of *Dracula* (screenplay by James V. Hart), but the impact of Dracula's demise is again diminished, this time by the film's insistence on playing Dracula's relationship with Mina as a genuine love story and trying to give Dracula's death a tragic tone.

EXERCISE: *DRACULA*

As I hope I have illustrated, *Dracula* is a film with considerable structural problems. What would you do to correct some of these issues? How would you utilize Mina, Harker et al. in the first act to make their takeover of the story not so jarring? What role would you give Van Helsing to make him a more formidable opponent for Dracula? How would Renfield figure into your reworked second and third acts? How would your climax for this story play out to resolve the conflicts in a more dramatically satisfying way?

_____

_____

_____

_____

_____

_____

_____

_____

_____

_____

DUMB & DUMBER
(1994, 107 min.)

Screenplay by Peter Farrelly, Bennett Yellin,
and Bobby Farrelly

MOST SCREENWRITING BOOKS draw their storytelling examples from the canon of "great" films. Perhaps it is only a matter of time before *Dumb & Dumber* takes its place among the giants.* In the meantime, this "self-proclaimed no-brainer"

---

* Indeed, some people think it already has. In 2008, *Empire Magazine* ranked this film number 445 on its list of the 500 greatest films *of all time.*

(Leonard Maltin's *Movie & Video Guide*) can assist us in our study of story structure.

Comedy, as I will explain in Chapter Nine, *dispels fears*, and the fear being tackled here is the adolescent's perennial dread of being a total loser. This archetype is humor for privileged young people invited to enjoy cruel laughs at the expense of those "inferior" to themselves. It targets the same kind of audience that made *The Jerry Springer Show* a sensation. The Egri-style "premise" (or, if you're more of a McKee fan, the "controlling idea") is: "Once a loser, always a loser."

The screenplay for *Dumb & Dumber* is in many ways a structural catastrophe, but as with *Dracula*, the film's box office success and cultural staying power mock such liabilities — a sobering reminder that if a movie clicks with its audience, nothing else matters.

Analysis: Characters & Situation

Who are the characters? Thick-skulled Rhode Island buddies Lloyd and Harry (picture Bert and Ernie if they didn't get enough oxygen at birth) and the players in a kidnapping plot that turns into a cross-country chase when the two idiots become inadvertently involved.

What are the conflicts? When it comes to comedy, conflict is tricky. Make it too tame, and the audience falls asleep; too intense, and the humor dries up (it's hard to laugh when you're in fear for the characters' lives). Nevertheless, several identifiable conflicts drive *Dumb & Dumber*, even an internal struggle for one of the characters.

Conflict #1: THE KIDNAPPING PLOT. The engine that sets this whole circus train rolling is the kidnapping of the husband of Mary Swanson, a rich Colorado heiress. She's instructed to leave a briefcase full of ransom money in the Providence airport... but she ends up with Lloyd as her limo driver. He falls in lust at first sight and recovers the briefcase from the floor of the airport, thinking she left it by mistake. He talks his buddy Harry into traveling to Aspen ("where the beer flows like wine") to return the briefcase... and maybe get a chance to lift up the back of Mary's skirt while they're hugging. When the kidnappers (led by the master-mind Nicholas Andre) find out, they set out to recover the ransom money and kill Lloyd and Harry. Issue of conten-tion: *Will Lloyd and Harry get to Mary before the kidnappers find them and take the briefcase?*

Conflict #2: LLOYD AND HARRY VERSUS THE WORLD. The world can be a rough place with a combined IQ of 10, and throughout the film are moments in which Lloyd and Harry's natural stupidity makes their journey much more dif-ficult. They get robbed by a "sweet old lady on a motorized cart." Lloyd nearly gets raped in a bathroom stall by a burly redneck. Harry almost loses his tongue when it gets stuck to the metal frame of a ski lift. Time and again, the boys' lack of smarts works against them. At many moments in the film, the biggest threat to Lloyd and Harry is not the kidnappers, but themselves; indeed, the criminals sometimes seem to be in the story just so it actually resembles a story and not merely a string of unconnected gag sequences. The issue: *Will Lloyd and Harry's stupidity get the better of them?*

Conflict #3: LLOYD'S DILEMMA. Like many such charac-ters since the dawn of movies, Lloyd is an idiot with a dream, which he states in a teary-eyed speech near the end of the first act: "I'm tired of having to eke my way through life.* I'm tired of being a nobody. Most of all, I'm tired of having nobody." Lloyd, dim bulb that he is, wants to be a somebody and find the love of a good woman, and his cross-country adventure might be his only real chance to make that wish come true. Harry is along for the ride and shares in all the

---

* A nit to pick: How on earth does a moron know the phrase "eke my way through life"?

comic misadventures — but it's Lloyd's romantic longing and discontent with his life, a discontent Harry doesn't completely share, that gets the two of them on the road in the first place. The issue: *Will Lloyd finally get to be a "somebody" and find a woman to love?*

When are the conflicts defined, and in what manner? Conflict #2, Lloyd and Harry's stupidity, is already raging before the plot gets underway. In the opening scene, when limo driver Lloyd stops to ask a sexy woman for directions, he bumbles his come-on (when she tells him her accent is Austrian, he hits her with a galoot-like "G'day, mate!"), then nearly rolls his nose up in the car's automatic window. And the credits haven't even started. Forget the kidnapping; for these goons day-to-day life is a death-defying struggle.

Conflict #1 warms up when Lloyd scoops the ransom briefcase up from the airport floor, right under the noses of Nicholas' henchmen. The thugs search Lloyd and Harry's apartment and, finding no trace of the briefcase, pull the head off their pet parakeet as a warning about what's coming. (Naturally, they don't get the message, assuming their poor bird's head just fell off; after all, Harry says, "he was pretty old.") Still, this conflict doesn't truly kick in even when Lloyd and Harry decide to head to Aspen to return Mary's briefcase; they have no idea that the locked briefcase contains ransom money, and therefore are not consciously involved in the kidnapping plot. And it's almost another twenty minutes, thirty-seven minutes into the film (35% of the running time), until the conflict really hits, as Nicholas finally orders his henchmen to do whatever it takes to get rid of Lloyd and Harry and recover the briefcase. The battle lines, such as they are, are now drawn; like it or not, know it or not, Lloyd and Harry are headed for a showdown. But this locking of the conflict, happening so long after the natural act break of Lloyd and Harry's setting off to Aspen, means that the first-act curtain is smeared across some twenty minutes of screen time, making the locking of the conflict seem overdue and too narratively diffuse.

It is not any sense of life-or-death urgency about the briefcase that gets Lloyd and Harry on the road to Aspen. Remember, they don't yet know what's in that case. Rather, it's Lloyd's dissatisfaction with his sorry lot in life, expressed in the speech quoted above (eighteen minutes in; 17%), that gets him out on the road and after his one chance to be a somebody, with Harry just more or less along for the ride. (He's the one with the car... or dog; it's a long story). Conflict #3 defined... albeit with a level of clear-eyed introspection that we see from Lloyd at no other time in the film.

What is The Point of No Return? The first half of Act Two is taken up by the boys' trip to Aspen, which gives them ample opportunity to deal with both Conflicts #1 and #2. (#3 is only really addressed during a fantasy sequence in which Lloyd imagines his courtship of Mary, where he dazzles her with his fart-lighting abilities — hey, if you've only got one skill, you'd better milk it, right?) They pick up one of the kidnappers posing as a hitchhiker, and at a roadside diner, they inadvertently kill him by dosing him with ultra-hot peppers, aggravating his ulcer to fatal proportions. Harry later chats up a pretty female skier also on her way to Aspen; this completely random conversation will pay off later with regard to Conflict #1 in an unexpected, but slightly illogical way. And, of course, Conflict #2 is always there, as Harry gets set on fire, Lloyd gets his hamburger spit in by a redneck who later tries to violate him, and they both make a motorcycle cop accidentally drink from a beer bottle full of Lloyd's piss.

Then, fifty-two minutes into the film (49%), the screenplay introduces an entirely new conflict that's now on-and-off until the end, even though it's never been set up prior to this. While doing some of the driving Lloyd takes a wrong exit, and they soon find out that they've been driving almost a whole day in the wrong direction. They run out of gas, and furious, Harry storms off, planning to walk back to Rhode Island. The new conflict: LLOYD VERSUS HARRY. The issue: *Can these friends stay friends?* This conflict is temporarily solved by Lloyd's arrival on a ridiculously tiny motor scooter that they ride the rest of the way to Aspen.

When the boys finally arrive in Aspen fifty-seven minutes in (53%), they crash a charity benefit hosted by Mary and her family (who are trying to keep up appearances despite the kidnapping). This event finally, firmly unites Lloyd and Harry with Conflict #1; for the rest of the film, they will be dealing with characters connected to the kidnapping. The bad guys spot Lloyd and Harry at the party and, after the on-the-road death of their henchman, assume that they're dealing with criminal masterminds who are here to take them out, a notion reinforced when Lloyd accidentally kills a rare snowy owl with a flying champagne cork (the kidnappers read this as a "warning"). Of course, Lloyd and Harry still don't even know they're involved in a kidnapping plot, and the way they keep "cleverly" eluding Nicholas' traps leads him to think he's dealing with arch-criminals. This venerable comic device, that of the idiot who comes off as brilliant, is handled here in such a tired, off-hand way that it is difficult to focus on; to see it done well, treat yourself to Peter Sellers' last great film, *Being There*.

Another structural hiccup comes at the party when Mary strikes up an unlikely connection with Harry. He makes her laugh, takes her mind off her troubles, and they start hanging out, infuriating Lloyd and making this late-introduced subconflict, Lloyd versus Harry, the engine that drives much of the rest of the second act. We get to see Harry's burgeoning connection with Mary thwarted both by his own means (the tongue on the ski-lift pole) and by the schemes of his "buddy" Lloyd (who slips him a massive dose of a powerful laxative). But hey, wasn't this supposed to be a movie about a kidnapping? What the hell's going on here? And how do we reach a Point of No Return when the writers seem to have completely forgotten about their main conflict?

Well, finally, ninety-four minutes into the film (88%), Lloyd finally gets Mary alone and confesses his feelings... garbling his words so badly that he ends up telling her that he "desperately want(s) to make love to a schoolboy." He recovers slightly and gets his real feelings out. At this stage, with the kidnappers seemingly forgotten by the writers, we'll take any port in this structural storm, and Conflict #3 has reached its Point of No Return.

How are the conflicts resolved?... which Mary abruptly resolves by telling Lloyd that his chances of winning her are one in a billion. Still, that resolves the conflict for *us*, not for him; he thinks those are great odds ("So you're telling me there's a chance!").

Then, before Mary can leave with her briefcase, Nicholas bursts in with a gun and handcuffs Mary and Lloyd to the bed. Conflict #1 has taken over the film again in a big way. Nicholas is furious to find out that the briefcase now contains nothing but Lloyd and Harry's handwritten IOUs (they've spent all the money on hotel rooms, ridiculous ski-town wear, and a Lamborghini), and he's about to pull the trigger as Conflict #1 *finally* reaches its clear Point of No Return. But then Harry bumbles in with a gun of his own (!) and starts randomly shooting up the place. He's followed in by FBI agents, led by the pretty skier Harry met on the road. Turns out she's an agent who's been following them the whole time; apparently the FBI now requires its agents to drive across country in a station wagon with skis on the roof. Nicholas is arrested, and Mary's husband is freed. Ninety-eight minutes in (92%), Conflict #1 is resolved. The husband and wife are reunited... at the expense of Lloyd, who doesn't get the girl. But at least he takes it well. After all, he only *fantasizes* about grabbing an FBI guy's gun and riddling Mary's husband with bullets in front of her.

Still, as Lloyd heads for home, at least he definitely has somebody... his dimwitted pal Harry, who saved his life. Naturally, they've patched things up (the late-in-the-game subconflict resolved). But wait, what about Conflict #2, Lloyd and Harry's stupidity? Well, a busload of Hawaiian Tropic girls pulls up to our heroes (who now have no car and are walking home to Rhode Island), informing them that they're looking for two "oil boys" to grease them up before competitions. Well, they're in luck, Harry and Lloyd tell them. "There's a town about a mile up the road. I'm sure you'll find a couple of guys there." Conflict #2 remains unresolved. Once a loser, always a loser.

IN SUMMARY, *DUMB & DUMBER* botches its structure in several ways. First of all, the conflict-locking points are scattered so widely throughout the story that the first- and second-act breaks do not land solidly. Indeed, they never really congeal into the recognizable stages of a dynamic-structural conflict — not to mention that a good portion of the film's second half is taken up by a conflict that's not even present in the first half.*

Dumb & Dumber is useful to consider, however, because it illustrates a unique dramatic principle regarding comedy. Comedy is the only genre in which successful films are regularly produced where the characters *do not change* as a result of their experiences. Indeed, this feature is oftentimes the film's supreme joke. After all the craziness and potentially life-altering experiences the comic protagonists go through, they remain stupidly, blissfully themselves, and thus free to blunder through more such adventures in the future. So it is here. After everything Lloyd and Harry experience, they have nothing to show for it. Lloyd doesn't get the girl, they don't get the money, and they aren't even smart enough to see a golden (tan) opportunity when it drops in their laps. Nothing changes, nothing is learned. Lloyd and Harry remain the same as they ever were.

---

*Granted, you *can* get away with building the second half of your film around completely different issues than those addressed in your first act. But you have to be a structural wizard... or at least better at constructing your story than the guys who wrote *Dumb & Dumber*. We'll be discussing what is probably cinema's most famous and well-executed example of this structural gambit a little later in this chapter.

Only in comedy can the characters wind up right back where they started and still have it work for an audience. It might not result in a coherent story, but if we're laughing till we puke, hey, someone will always be ready to hold the bucket. And who's counting anything but ticket sales?

EXERCISE: *DUMB & DUMBER*
As we mentioned in discussing *Dumb & Dumber*, comedies can find success even with characters whose experiences do not change them. Can you think of any successful films in other genres in which the characters do not change? An action film, a science fiction picture, even a straight drama? Write about two of these films below. What keeps the characters from changing, and why do those characters still work dramatically in spite of this lack of change?

Film #1 _____
How it Works _____
_____
_____

Film #2 _____
How it Works _____
_____

INVASION OF THE BODY SNATCHERS
(1956, 80 min.)

Screenplay by Daniel Mainwaring
Based on the *Collier's Magazine* serial
"The Body Snatchers" by Jack Finney

INVASION OF THE BODY SNATCHERS is one of the most influential science fiction films of all time. It has inspired three "official" remakes, and elements of it can be found in count-less other sci-fi films in the nearly sixty years since its release. It is also one of my personal all-time favorite movies and, in my view, the greatest horror film ever made, because its monster is an *abstraction*.

Think of the monster in every other horror movie. What does it do to you? It eats you. It slices you up. It possesses you. Crunch, chop, boo! You're gone. But in *Body Snatchers*, nothing visible happens to the evil force's prey. The threat is something *vague*, something about emotions – we lose them, or something. And it scares the living daylights out of you! This threat's very insubstantiality allows us to read any formless hor-ror into what's going on. What's at risk is our own extinction, happening behind our backs, as it were. And sleep – normally a healer – is the enemy.

Analysis: Characters and Situation

Who are the characters? Small-town doctor Miles Bennell, his once-and-future girlfriend, Becky Driscoll, and their unsuspect-ing friends and neighbors, who are being replaced by soulless trespassers from outer space.

When is it? 1956, the year of the film's release. America had, at this point in its history, achieved status as a kind of "promised land" of economic security and consensus values. Small-town life was still a reality for most Americans – your present author lived it himself. And yet, this way of life was menaced by strange threats that hung over our lives: the atomic bomb, Communism, most of all — *the future*, which promised to be unfamiliar in the extreme. ("So much has been discovered these last few years," the film's hero says, "anything is possible.") It was the last time in our history that we had any hope of hanging onto an old-fashioned, understandable way of life, and it did not last much longer. *Invasion of the Body Snatchers* senses this impending obliteration of all that is familiar and comforting, and the film wants desperately to hold onto what we have. It is nostalgic for its own time.

What is the conflict? *Invasion of the Body Snatchers* is a movie that wears its conflict on its sleeve. It's a classic "us versus them" sci-fi story, with Miles, a stand-in for all of humanity, battling the alien invaders. The conflict is external and easily summed up: Miles wants to escape from the town of Santa Mira to warn the world of the encroaching takeover, while the aliens want to turn Miles into one of them, then subjugate all of humanity in the same way. The conflict: HUMANITY VERSUS THE INVADERS. The "Issue": *the very fate of mankind.*

But before it tips its hand and reveals itself as an invaders-from-space story, the film teases us that the main conflict may be an internal one — namely that the people of Santa Mira may be suffering from a "mass hysteria," making them believe their loved ones are not who they appear to be. It's as if the whole town needs a psychiatrist, and it's not until Miles and his friends stumble upon hatching alien pods that we are certain that the invasion is real and not just a fabrication of overwrought psyches.

Many critics read *Invasion of the Body Snatchers* as an allegory on McCarthy-era paranoia, a reflection of widespread fears that a covert Communist infiltration was threatening the very fabric of American life. After all, the film's "pod people," like the Communists, "look just like us." But the film ultimately exists independently of any allegorical readings, and is driven forward by its strong external conflict.

When is the conflict defined, and in what manner? *Invasion of the Body Snatchers* has a singular structure, consisting of a slow build followed by a series of escalating *revelatory shocks*, as the characters discover first the existence of the pods, then the extent of their control over the town. (This escalating shock structure works thanks to a concept known as "hedonic adaptation," which I will be discussing in detail in Chapter Ten.)

THE SETUP: Returning from a medical convention, Miles is struck by the bizarre behavior of his friends and neighbors. Little Jimmy Grimaldi insists that his mother is not his mother; cousin Wilma just knows that Uncle Ira is not himself. Then, in an odd reversal, Miles' patients suddenly decide that their problems are no longer worth bothering the doctor with. They're healthy again. *Too healthy.*

REVELATORY SHOCK #1: Things don't get really strange, though, until twenty minutes into the film (25% of the running time), when Miles' writer friend, Jack Belicec, finds a body on his pool table. This "body" is bizarrely generic, with unformed features and no fingerprints, but it rapidly evolves (while Jack sleeps) into a perfect replica of Jack himself, right down to a fresh cut on his hand. Soon, another body, this one a half-formed replica of Miles' ex-girlfriend Becky, shows up in the Driscolls' basement. But before Miles and company can get these bodies to the police, they both disappear. It's beginning to look like mass hysteria after all... but something weird is definitely going on. At exactly the one-quarter mark, the characters are now immersed in the conflict that will dictate the rest of the film's action.

What is The Point of No Return? REVELATORY SHOCK #2: Then, at the forty-minute mark (exactly 50% of the way through the film), Miles finds giant alien pods hatching in his greenhouse. There are four of them: replicas of Becky, Jack and his wife, and Miles himself. Finally, at this moment, it's clear what's happening. The people of Santa Mira are being insidiously replaced by creatures not of this earth, and Miles and his friends must escape and warn the world before it's too late.

REVELATORY SHOCK #3: They try to telephone the FBI in Los Angeles, the closest big city. This was before the days of direct dialing, which means they have to go through a human (they hope!) operator, but when the courteous voice informs them that all lines out of town are busy, they realize that Santa Mira's telephone exchange has been taken over by the invaders (forty-five minutes in; 56%).

REVELATORY SHOCK #4: The question now becomes, *how much* of the town is under the pods' control? This make-or-break question is answered the next morning, when the characters witness farmers doling out truckloads of pods in the town center in broad daylight, under the direction of the local police, for distribution to the outlying communities. The aliens have reached the break-out threshold, and are ready to become "a malignant disease spreading through the whole country." Fifty-seven minutes into the film (71%), it's The Point of No Return moment. If the heroes don't do something fast, mankind as they know it is doomed.

How is the conflict resolved? REVELATORY SHOCK #5: The shocks are coming thick and fast now. Fifty-eight minutes in (73%), Jack and his wife succumb to the pods and betray Miles and Becky. With the "pod people" in pursuit, they evade capture and run like mad for the main highway. As darkness falls, Miles and Becky hide in a tunnel outside town. Popping bennies, they struggle to stay awake, because the pods grow while you sleep. Then they *absorb your mind*, though only parts of it; the *emotions* get left behind with the husk of your old body, obsolete appendages of the human animal, unnecessary to the vegetable lives of the pod spawn.

REVELATORY SHOCK #6: During the night, Miles leaves the desperately exhausted Becky unattended for a moment. Then, overcome with emotion, he kisses her... *and realizes that he's not kissing Becky*. She fell asleep, and now she's an alien (seventy-five minutes in; 94%). Miles is the only human left in Santa Mira, and the fate of the world rests on his shoulders.

With the pods at his heels, Miles finally makes it to the highway, where he tries to stop cars, screaming his warning: "They're already here! You're next!" But, to his horror, he sees trucks laden with pods bound for L.A., San Francisco, and other major cities. The conflict is technically unresolved, but it looks like curtains for the human race...

AND THAT'S HOW THE FILM was *supposed* to end. As it was released, however, *Invasion of the Body Snatchers* has a framing story with a ranting Miles ("I'm not insane!") being dragged into a hospital. He is interrogated by a psychiatrist, who hears the main story as a flashback. At the end, with Miles' story told, the doctor is on the verge of committing him to an asylum when an ambulance attendant brings in an injured truck driver he just found buried under "the most peculiar things I've ever seen" – gigantic pods! Believing Miles at last, the doctor calls "every law enforcement agency in the state," plus the FBI — and Miles, for the first time, looks hopeful. He's no longer alone against the menace. The conflict is still not completely resolved. The pods are still out there. But Miles has accomplished his goal. The authorities have been warned, and the human race just might be saved after all.

As commentators frequently note, this prologue and epilogue were imposed on screenwriter Daniel Mainwaring and director Don Siegel by the studio. *Body Snatchers'* original, more nihilistic finale, with Miles helplessly shouting his warnings at passing cars, offered the audience no hope at all. Although the framing device has been criticized (notably by Siegel himself) as an artistic blemish on the film, I consider it an enhancement that adds intrigue and suspense to the opening, and hope to the ending. Critics claim that it adulterates the terror because it indicates that the human race is going to win out. But when I first saw it, I didn't think that mankind's victory was a shoo-in by any stretch. Rather, humanity was now facing a great war with an uncertain outcome, so this epilogue scared the bejabbers out of me. Without the hope that it held out, I would have fallen into an unhappy dejection. I would have known that the filmmaker was not my friend.

EXERCISE: *INVASION OF THE BODY SNATCHERS*
Invasion of the Body Snatchers works by using "revelatory shocks," moving the story forward through moments that increase the threat and build the terror of its narrative. Name another film that likewise builds its story through the use of these revelatory shocks, and describe in detail the ways in which these shocks move the story forward and increase the tension and suspense. (It doesn't have to be a horror film, of course, just one that uses this device in a similar way.)

Revelatory-Shock Film _____
_____

How the Shocks Are Used _____
_____
_____
_____
_____
_____
_____
_____

KING LEAR
(approx. 1605; 140 pages in the Pelican edition)

Play written by William Shakespeare

KING LEAR IS IMPORTANT to our investigation because, like all of Shakespeare's plays, it is a *five-act* drama. How will this translate into our three-acts-with-a-conflict structure? Will it do so at all?

The subtexts of *Lear*, understandably, have just about been analyzed to death. Our purpose here is simply to see if the play fits into three-acts-with-a-conflict. If it doesn't, that's no reflection of *Lear*, or even of five-act formats. My system is not meant to encompass all great art, but rather to provide a sort of base minimum, a default or fall-back below which the dramatist probably would not wish to slip.

Analysis: Characters and Situation

Who are the characters? Lear, aged king of ancient Britain; his daughters (the duplicitous Goneril and Regan, and the noble Cordelia); and assorted members of the British court.

What are the conflicts? Interestingly, *King Lear* contains little in the way of internal conflict. Characters' emotional attitudes are fairly circumscribed from the start (Lear's inflexible pride, Goneril and Regan's treachery), and they don't vacillate much during the course of the action. If a character does undergo an emotional reversal (like the blinded Gloucester's acceptance of his previously forsaken son Edgar), that change happens with such minimal soul-searching that it plays more as a plot twist than as a manifestation of a personality struggle.

Lear starts out foolish and gains wisdom; however, the play drops a number of hints that he was a good king prior to his folly in the opening scene. Evidently his "tell me how much you love me" lunacy is a transient lapse in judgment. He has one bad moment, which unfortunately leads to the decimation of his kingship and his family. It's classical tragedy at its most basic, but Lear's downfall is prompted less by a major personality flaw than by one isolated bad decision. The change isn't from bad king to good king; the real change seems to be that he learns humility. So, even though the play bears his name, Lear's personality change is not the core point of the story.* Still, it does get the ball rolling plot-wise, so... Conflict #1: LEAR'S PRIDE.

---

* Of course, Lear also starts out alive and ends up dead, and there is no bigger character change than that.

Lear scarcely needs internal discord, however, because the play swarms with external conflicts. Nearly every character harbors a vendetta against someone else in the story. Plots and treachery are rife. Lear clashes with Cordelia when she refuses to show him the submissive flattery he demands, then with Goneril and Regan when they expel him from their castle and strip him of his retinue of soldiers. Gloucester's bastard son, Edmund, covets his legitimate brother Edgar's birthright, so he pits his father against his brother by making it seem that "the legitimate" intends patricide, then follows through by turning the king's evil daughters and their husbands against Gloucester as well. Later, Goneril and Regan conspire against each other for Edmund's favors. There's so much thrust-and-parry going on, it's natural to assume that one of these external conflicts must be the engine driving the action forward. Conflict #2: EVERYONE VERSUS EVERYONE ELSE. The "issue" was put best on the poster for another classic tragedy cited on page 33, *The Texas Chain Saw Massacre*: *"Who will survive and what will be left of them?"*

These conflicts, however, are all spurred on by the fundamentally flawed nature of Shakespeare's universe, the ill will of angry gods bearing down on his hapless creations. Gloucester describes the horrors in Act I, Scene 2: "These late eclipses in the sun and moon portend no good to us... Love cools, friendship falls off, brothers divide. In cities, mutinies; in countries, discord; in palaces, treason; and the bond cracked 'twixt son and father. Machinations, treachery, and all ruinous disorders follow us disquietly to our graves." All of these tragedies (and more) come to bear on the characters of *King Lear*. Fathers turn against their children (either spitefully, like Lear, or as a result of being hoodwinked, like Gloucester), who likewise attack their parents. Kingdoms are torn asunder, the innocent die, the wicked are punished too little or too late. At all turns, these disasters are blamed not so much on the infelicitous actions of the characters themselves, but on fate, the harsh judgments of a dissatisfied Providence. The play is driven by a titanic rift in the universe's sense of justice, logic, and decency, a rift that has altered the play's world so violently that only the king's fool can make any sense of it. Conflict #3: MAN VERSUS THE FATES. Issue of contention: *Can man master his own destiny, or is he a helpless victim of the will of the gods?*

How are the conflicts defined, and in what manner? In his introduction to the Pelican edition of *King Lear*, Stephen Orgel writes that over the course of Shakespeare's first two acts (61 pages out of 138 in the Pelican edition, or 44% of the play's length), "Once the enabling actions of the opening two scenes have occurred, the tragedy takes shape with extraordinary swiftness. Lear's reduction from monarch to 'a poor old man / As full of grief as age, wretched in both' (II. 4. 272–273) is complete by the end of Act II, the blinding of Gloucester by the end of Act III."[19]

Shakespeare lays out his main plots in the first two scenes of the play's first act (of five), and swiftly establishes both Conflicts #1 and #2. Lear splits his kingdom between daughters Goneril and Regan, who reward him by conspiring to overthrow him. With equal ill judgment, the old king banishes Cordelia, his only truly loving daughter, and Kent, his most devoted courtier. Meanwhile, Edmund plots against *his* father and brother by making it appear that one is scheming against the other. As these stratagems unfold, it initially seems that the catastrophes looming on the horizon are occasioned solely by Lear's stubborn pride, his daughters' treacherous natures, and Edmund's embrace of evil. But when Gloucester reads his letter from "Edgar," he blames the heavens for the mounting troubles (as quoted above). Here, at the sixty-two-page mark, Conflict #3, the idea of the universe's looming caprice is introduced, and will be reiterated throughout the play as events grow increasingly bleak and deadly.

What is The Point of No Return? Through Shakespeare's first three acts, we watch helplessly as events close in on Lear,

---

[19] From Stephen Orgel's introduction to *The Pelican Shakespeare: King Lear – The 1608 Quarto and 1623 Folio Texts* (New York: Penguin Putnam, 2000), XXXIX.

Gloucester, and the other characters we care about. Cast out by his daughters, Lear is reduced to screaming at a storm. Kent is clamped in the stocks. Edgar is forced, under fear for his life, to masquerade as an insane beggar, and Gloucester is tricked into persecuting him, ever unaware that Edmund is scheming against them both. The fates certainly seem aligned against our protagonists, but at this point, none of the evils that have been heaped on them is irreversible. Goneril and Regan could still conceivably mend their ways. Gloucester and Edgar might reconcile, as might Lear and Cordelia. Hope still stirs within us.

That hope is shattered at the end of Shakespeare's Act III, when Regan and her husband, the Duke of Cornwall, gouge out Gloucester's eyes: "Out, vile jelly!" (p. 87, 63%). Now an irreparable wrong has been done: Gloucester, an innocent man, is mutilated. From here on out, we expect only the worst for these characters from the gods that plague them, as the play moves toward its overwhelmingly tragic conclusion.

How are the conflicts resolved? Many critics and Shakespeare scholars regard *King Lear* as the Bard's most pessimistic work. There is a good reason for that: *The central conflict is not resolved* — which is not to say that the individual stories are likewise left up in the air. Lear is reunited with his one loyal daughter, Cordelia, who has returned with the French army to drive Goneril and Regan from Britain. The two evil sisters, meanwhile, have been jostling to marry Edmund (who is the new Duke of Gloucester now that he has essentially destroyed his father). Goneril poisons Regan, then, wracked with guilt (finally!), stabs herself. Edgar at last asserts himself, kills his bastard brother in a duel, and reclaims his birthright. Meanwhile, Cordelia is captured by the English forces and hanged before her execution order can be rescinded, and Lear, mad with grief over this loss, dies of a broken heart.

From a purely narrative perspective, tidy enough. The various subconflicts that make up Conflict #2 have been resolved (for better or, more often, for worse), and Lear has certainly learned his lesson about the dangers of pride. But nothing has been resolved thematically. Evil has been punished, yes, but good has not been rewarded. Lear and Cordelia are dead, Gloucester blinded for life, and Kent left to pay lone, miserable witness to the death of his master and an innocent woman. Though the noble Edgar claims the British throne, he is aware that his victory is a Pyrrhic one and that he remains at the mercy of the gods ("The weight of this sad time we must obey.") The play ends on a note not of renewed hope for the kingdom, but of woe for the innocent dead and of knowledge that their senseless demises can never be adequately recompensed. Nothing of past glories remains, only despair and the pathetic semblance of restored order. *King Lear* ends as it began, with man at the mercy of a cruel and indifferent universe, one whose attitude is best summed up by poor, blind Gloucester in Act IV, Scene 1: "As flies to wanton boys are we to the gods / They kill us for their sport."

WE OBSERVE THAT THE THREE-ACT DYNAMIC STRUCTURE does fit *King Lear*, but Shakespeare's own five-act structure has its function as well. Shakespeare lays *Lear* out like this:

ACT I: 5 scenes; 36 pages; 26% of the play; ends with Lear sending Kent to Regan's castle with a letter

ACT II: 4 scenes; 27 pages; 20% of the play; ends with Lear quarreling with Goneril and Regan and fleeing into a storm rather than dismiss his knights

ACT III: 7 scenes; 25 pages; 18% of the play; ends with Gloucester blinded by Cornwall, who is then killed by one of his own servants

ACT IV: 7 scenes; 31 pages; 22% of the play; ends with Lear's reunion with Cordelia

ACT V: 3 scenes; 20 pages; 14% of the play; ends with Edgar killing Edmund, Regan and Goneril dying, Cordelia being executed, and Lear dying of a broken heart

Robert McKee discusses Shakespearean five-act structure, explaining that in movies the five-act "rhythm" requires "a major reversal every fifteen or twenty minutes." He warns: "When the writer multiplies acts, he's forcing the invention of five, perhaps six, seven, eight, nine or more brilliant scenes... Even if the writer feels he's up to creating a major reversal every fifteen minutes, turning act climaxes on scenes of life and death, life and death, life and death, life and death, life and death, seven or eight times over, boredom sets in."[20]

Sure does. But not if Shakespeare's at the wheel. With the exception of Act I, each act of the play climaxes with a major, game-changing event in the play's narrative, with the most catastrophic (The Point of No Return) coming at almost exactly the two-thirds point of the play's running time. Act V, even though it is the shortest and contains the fewest scenes, deftly resolves the play's various conflicts and sends our characters to their fates, happy or (mostly) otherwise. Thus, even though Shakespeare chose a five-act structure, three-act dynamic structure can be superimposed on the existing play, and the structural model fits like a glove, with no twists necessary to make it work.

Hmm. You know... Shakespeare might have made a hell of a screenwriter.

---

[20] McKee, *Story*, 220–222.

EXERCISE: *KING LEAR*

King Lear, like all of Shakespeare's plays, conforms to a five-act structure. Choose two films that likewise have a more-than-three-act narrative structure, and outline the act breaks below. Even with these additional acts, do these films still conform to the conflict-locking, Point-of-No-Return, conflict-resolution scheme of dynamic structure?

Film #1 _____

Number of Acts _____

Act Breaks and Times of Act Break Occurrence _____

_____

_____

_____

Dynamic-Structure Locking of Conflict _____

_____

Dynamic-Structure Point of No Return _____

_____

Dynamic-Structure Resolution of Conflict _____

_____

Film #2 _____

Number of Acts _____

Act Breaks and Times of Act Break Occurrence _____

_____

_____

_____

Dynamic-Structure Locking of Conflict _____

_____

Dynamic-Structure Point of No Return _____

_____

Dynamic-Structure Resolution of Conflict _____

_____

LAWRENCE OF ARABIA
(1962; 216 minutes in the restored version)

Screenplay by Robert Bolt and Michael Wilson*
Based on *The Seven Pillars of Wisdom* by T. E. Lawrence

IN HIS ESSAY "THE BIBLE AS LITERATURE," Prof. Leland Ryken defines the epic as "a long narrative of national destiny,"[21] and David Lean's amazing biopic *Lawrence of Arabia*, which tells the story of Arabia's quest for self-determination during World War I, certainly fits this description. But *Lawrence of Arabia* is not your garden-variety epic. The screenplay eschews the often-simplistic characterizations of large-scale Hollywood blockbusters to render a complex portrait of an enigmatic historical figure who, rather than being swept up in the film's conflicts or even causing them, *embodies* them. As a result, our look at this film will be somewhat more involved and far-ranging in its structure than our study of the previous pictures. It may be rough going at first, but as with the film itself, bear with me. I'm building to something here.

Analysis: Characters and Situation

Who are the characters? T. E. Lawrence, the real-life British officer who fought with the tribes of Arabia against the Turks in the First World War, and his various allies and enemies, Briton, Arab, and Turk.

What are the conflicts? Like other war films, *Lawrence of Arabia* is full of strong conflicts among characters and groups of characters that make up the various factions in the war. The Arab tribes

---

* Due to his status as a blacklisted writer, Michael Wilson was uncredited on the original theatrical release of *Lawrence*; his credit was restored by the Writers Guild of America in 1978.

[21] Leland Ryken, Ph.D., "The Bible as Literature," in *The Origin of the Bible*, ed. Philip Wesley Comfort (Carol Stream, IL: Tyndale House, 2004), 132.

have ruled over the desert lands that provide the film's setting (almost another character, really) since time immemorial. Now, the marauding Turks are threatening their domain, and the Arabs are ready to fight back. The British have come to support the Arabs in war and, many of the Arabs believe, to divide Arabia between themselves and their European allies once the fighting is over. (It is never really explained how Lawrence, a man who seems so temperamentally unsuited for combat, would find himself in the thick of a war, or even why he would have joined the army in the first place. But as the film progresses, we learn that Lawrence is never quite what he seems). Conflict #1: WORLD WAR I. The issue: *Who will win the war?*

In addition to the war between the British/Arab alliance and the Turks, numerous points of tension resonate between the British, who see the Arabs as savages needing to learn the ways of "civilized" (white English) rule, and the Arabs, who view the British, not without reason, as potential colonizers. There are also clashes among the individual Arab tribes, who have been at each other's throats for centuries. This infighting is exemplified by the hostilities between Sherif Ali, the proud noble of the Hareth tribe, and Auda Abu Tayi, fierce chieftain of the Hawitat people. Conflict #2: ALLIES AT ODDS. The issue: *Who will control Arabia once the war is over?*

Lawrence himself is frequently at odds with the film's other characters. There is tension with his commanding officers in the British army, who see him as a mercurial, unstable rogue whom they nevertheless tolerate because he gets results. Lawrence also butts heads with his Arab allies, notably Ali, who never knows whether in Lawrence he is dealing with the holy savior of Arabia, another bloodthirsty tyrant, or a flat-out madman. Conflict #3: LAWRENCE VERSUS THE OTHERS. The issue: *Will Lawrence have his way, or will other ideas defeat his own?*

Then, of course, there are the conflicts that rage within Lawrence himself. Many film characters embody dualistic inner conflicts, but the problem here is that there aren't just two Lawrences, but several. Still, if you squint, they sort of lump into two, in a very general kind of way. First, there is the Lawrence who wants to stay in Arabia, the "desert-loving Englishman" who comes to see himself as a conqueror, indeed as something like a god. Then you have the Lawrence who just wants to escape his trial in the desert, the Lawrence who realizes that "any man is what I am." Conflict #4: LAWRENCE VERSUS LAWRENCE. The issue: *Just who is this guy anyway, and who does he think he is?*

So, we have a nice range of conflicts here, external and internal. Nevertheless, analyzing *Lawrence of Arabia* proves elusive. There are plenty of conflicts, sure, but which one is the main one, the straw that stirs the sand, so to speak? Lawrence versus his British superiors? Lawrence versus the Turks? Lawrence versus the desert? Lawrence versus *himself*? Conflicts are all over the place. The question is, which one escalates to irreversibility at the two-thirds mark of the film, and then resolves itself at the end? And the answer, as I will illustrate in the remainder of this chapter… is none of them. Every time I attempted to foreground one of these conflicts as the principal driver of the action, the film threw me a curve that ultimately prevented any of these conflicts from paying off and resolving the film in an unambiguous way.

How are the conflicts defined, and in what manner, *and* what is The Point of No Return?

Conflict #1: This conflict needs no real narrative setup. As a lieutenant in His Majesty's service, Lawrence is against the Turks from the start, and all of the military campaigns carried out in the course of the film are part of this conflict.

The Point of No Return for this conflict arrives 169 minutes into the film (77% of the running time), when Lawrence has an ugly run-in with a Turkish bey who tortures and (it is implied) rapes him. After this experience, Lawrence's duty-bound opposition to the Turks turns personal and nasty, an enmity that reaches its peak in the bloody battle outside Damascus ("No prisoners!").

Nevertheless, the war with the Turks can't be the main conflict, primarily because the *audience* is never really asked to harbor a major grudge against them. Even after Lawrence is abused by the bey, our main issue is how this treatment has changed Lawrence, not how the Turks will be punished for inflicting this brutality on him. Really, we have almost no feelings at all about the Turks, who with the exception of the bey, are mostly seen as an armed, faceless horde. They are the film's straw men, and whenever Lawrence is warring against them, he's really warring with some aspect of himself.

Conflict #2: The conflicts amongst the different allied factions of the war likewise cannot be foregrounded, largely because Lawrence, the film's protagonist, is not the primary actor driving these conflicts forward. The British and Arabs harbored deep-seated resentments and grudges against one another long before Lawrence set foot in the desert, and though he is forced to be a spokesman for British interests in Arabia, he doesn't take to it with any particular zeal (a problem that worsens when his British superiors begin to perceive him as far too attached to the interests of his "Arab friends").

The Point of No Return for this conflict arrives 201 minutes in (93%), when the war is over. The Arabs hold the capital city of Damascus, and the various tribes are now in a position where they must learn to cooperate with one another to forge an Arab state, or face subjugation to British colonials. But the Arabs, at war with one another even longer than they've been at war with potential British colonizing interests, cannot forge a true compromise, and

Lawrence is helpless to affect real change. He does his best, but he's trapped between the British position, which he is beholden to despite his true feelings, and the Arabs, with whom he sympathizes but with whom he can never truly be one. The film ends with these conflicts still raging, and with Lawrence's pathetic efforts at conciliation proving utterly ineffective.

Conflict #3: Lawrence versus his superiors is a nonstarter for the film's main conflict. Sure, Lawrence frequently battles his commanding officers, who bristle at the major's unorthodox methods. Still, he undeniably gets the job done, so they can't dismiss him, much as they may desire to do so. Lawrence, likewise, knows that without the dictates of the commanders, he has no real jurisdiction in Arabia and would likely not even be allowed back into the country. So this conflict ultimately results in a sort of uneasy stalemate, like an unhappily married couple staying together "for the children" (in this case, the war effort).

Lawrence's conflict with the Arabs is of a different character. They are at first suspicious of this blonde-haired, blue-eyed would-be savior who has come to lead them through the desert like Moses (his own analogy). He, likewise, is critical of the Arabs, whose hidebound prejudices and inability to compromise has rendered them "a little people, a silly people" in the eyes of the world. Soon, though, he wins them over, first by donning Arabian garb and learning the ways of the desert, then by defying the dictates of their cultural lore by crossing the harshest part of the desert and attacking a Turkish sea base from the land. It seems that Lawrence has truly "gone native"... until his rape at the hands of the bey (The Point of No Return for this conflict as well) reminds him of how non-native he is. This occurrence, as much as his inability to broker a true compromise among the Arab tribes after their victory in the war, reminds him that he can never be an Arab. So, if this issue is the main conflict of the film, Lawrence basically loses.

Conflict #4: From the earliest scenes in the film, it is clear that Lawrence is an unruly fit wherever he finds himself. In the "fat country" of England, he's obviously "different," a slim, dreamy-eyed, hard-to-read figure who descends into Arabia like some sort of mystical angel (complete with white robes) and attempts to conquer the land that no man can tame. Over and over again, however, Lawrence does what "it is written" that no one can do: He makes his way out of the blistering Nephud Desert alive, and he leads his troops to Aqaba and attacks the Turks from the land. When his British commanders flatly inform him that this strategy is impossible to execute, he replies, "Yes. I know it's impossible. I did it." (This remark is consistent with the epic's frequent inclusion of "a central epic feat performed by the epic hero, a feat that usually involves military conquest"[22]). By the film's second half, postintermission, Lawrence's self-image has inflated to gargantuan proportions; he parades on top of a train like a warrior god and even invites his men to walk on water with him.

The Point of No Return here, as with Conflicts #1 and #3, is Lawrence's torture by the Turkish bey. He is reminded most brutally that he is just a man, and one who can never truly rule the desert and its people. He begs to be released from his Arab obligations, but the British high command insists that he is too valuable and sends him back into the thick of it. So, rather than being a benevolent ruler of the land and people he loves, he decides to try the route of a tyrant, leading a bloody attack against Turkish soldiers outside Damascus. (We have already seen that Lawrence has a covert taste for bloodshed; when forced earlier in the film

---

[22] Ryken, 132.

to execute a treacherous Arab, he confesses, disturbed, that he liked pulling the trigger). He is frightened and confused by what he has become, and peace gives him no more solace than war, as his inability to broker a compromise does nothing but remind him that he does not belong there. He is sent home to nothing, an Englishman who doesn't feel at home in England and an "Arab" who is not truly welcome in the desert. Another conflict, another nonresolution.

SO I DISCOVERED FAIRLY EARLY ON that, in attempting to analyze this film using my dynamic-structural system, nothing seemed quite right. The story upon which I was attempting to impose this system seemed deeply chaotic; indeed, none of the conflicts that I established seemed to resolve in a clean and satisfactory way. I was forced, therefore, to change my assumptions.

I began by looking at the end of the movie, to see what the climactic scene was about, what story element was resolved, or at least what the film was attempting to resolve. I found that this scene was a shouting match in which Lawrence tries, and fails, to induce the assembled Arab clans to create a postwar pan-Arab union. Because this event is the film's climax, I hazarded a guess that this conflict — Lawrence's quest to bring about Arab unity (which was already present as an aspect of my dynamic-structural Conflict #3) — is what the film is really about.

I then backtracked through the movie and, sure enough, the film is rife with scenes that address the issue of "Arab unity"; it is a consistent theme throughout. The principal stumbling block to Lawrence's achieving this goal is the Arabs themselves, that is, cultural traits that stand in the way of transtribal unity. Sound familiar? This read is beginning to feel like a Howard-and-Mabley-style breakdown of the film. So, let's try this their way and see what we get.

The Conflict: Lawrence versus Arab Disunity

As you may recall, Howard and Mabley define conflict as "Somebody wants something badly and is having difficulty getting it." Lawrence wants Arab unity, and trying to get it gives him nothing but difficulties.

According to H & M's dynamic, the things frustrating the protagonist's attempts to achieve his goal are collectively known as obstacles. The obstacle in Lawrence's path is *a complex of Arab cultural attitudes that threaten unity in a variety of ways.*

Finally, there is H & M's three-act dynamic, the key moment of which is the *culmination*, "the high or low point of the screenplay, the event toward which all that precedes is driving" — which concludes their Act Two (and corresponds, more or less, to my Point of No Return).

Let's break it down:

Act One "*sets up the overriding conflict.*" Lawrence wants Arab unity and is having trouble getting it.

Act Two "*consists of a series of obstacles which together can be summed up: 'Will the protagonist stand up for him/herself?', and concludes with the Culmination, thus creating a new tension, stated as 'What will happen?'*" When he first attempts to unite the Arabs, Lawrence has quite a task ahead of him, as the Arabs don't see themselves as a unified people: "The Arabs? What tribe is that?" Auda derides Lawrence ninety-two minutes into the film (43%). Against all odds, Lawrence unites the tribes and leads them to victory at Aqaba, but after many subsequent triumphs, he hits a low point at 159 minutes (74%). Over the course of the film, the further from reach Lawrence's goals seem, the more unrealistic he becomes about his own powers — so he undertakes a supremely unrealistic effort by entering the Turk-held city of Deraa alone, and is captured and tortured.

Act Three "*leads directly (with twists and turns) from the second-act Culmination to the Resolution of the overriding conflict.*" A now-disillusioned and embittered Lawrence launches a blood vendetta against the Turks. Rallying the meanest Arabs he can find — murderers with prices on their heads — he achieves victory on the battlefield (albeit through ruthless means), but at the postwar pan-Arab conference, Lawrence is unable to rectify the age-old differences among the tribes. In the end, the original obstacles prove insurmountable; Lawrence's goal ultimately eludes him.

Lawrence of Arabia is a difficult film to analyze Howard-and-Mabley-style because the issue that provides the dramatic spine of the story according to this system — a man struggling against a complex of recalcitrant cultural norms — is the least arresting thing in the film. So much else is going on in the narrative, so many powerful ideas and scenes, that the issue of Arabian disunity registers on the viewer as little more than a passing nuisance, even though it is, in fact, the core dynamic that drives, or at least should be driving, the story. In fact, on my first pass through the film with a stopwatch, I didn't even bother taking any notes about Arab unity. Yes, it's important, but ho-hum. A lot of the most dramatic scenes in *Lawrence* have nothing to do with this issue, making it hard to believe that this tension is what actually drives the story. But it's the only narrative element that plays out over three acts with a Point of No Return and a real (albeit anticlimactic) resolution. If this element isn't *Lawrence's* main conflict, then the film doesn't really have one.

It's pretty clear that, for a story about unity, *Lawrence* isn't very well unified. In a well-structured story, every scene addresses the core conflict in some way. This focus harkens back to Aristotle's unity of action. So, *Lawrence* honestly isn't very well structured (*Gasp! Did I say that?*). Indeed, the film sags considerably between 152 and 166 minutes, 70–76% of the film's running time. There is always a price to be paid for indulging in scenes that are off the film's main point, and that price is the audience's attention. All the razzle-dazzle in the world can't sustain a viewer's fascination if he has no clear idea what to focus on, and such a film eventually grows tedious. It does pick up again by the end, but that fifteen minutes is wearisome to wade through.

WELL, THAT'S HOWARD AND MABLEY. Maybe one of our other gurus would work better. What would Lajos Egri say about this one?

Egri defines *four types of conflict*, only two of which are useful in writing drama: *slowly rising conflicts*, which build tension to a breaking point at the climax, and *"foreshadowing" conflicts*, whereby tensions between characters or knowledge of past events come to a head as the story moves to its climax. *Lawrence's* conflict, Lawrence against Arab disunity, would seem to be the slowly rising kind. But how does knowing that help us?

Let's see if breaking this situation down into acts (or, as Egri calls them, "movements") does any good...

Egri's Three Movements

(1) *CRISIS in the antagonists' lives, which grows in intensity*
Crisis: Arab disunity

(2) *CLIMAX, when everything comes to a head and the two forces meet in their most naked and aggressive opposition*
Unable to hold the tribes together, Lawrence tries to bring about unity all by himself, and is raped for his effort. In the grand scheme, though, this event barely qualifies as a climax, as the melting away of the tribes is hardly a "naked and aggressive opposition" — not to mention that the rape belongs to the Lawrence-versus-the-Turks conflict anyway.

(3) *RESOLUTION, where the victor emerges from the conflict triumphant, and the premise has been proven*

In spite of Lawrence's best efforts, the pan-Arab conference fails to unite the tribes. The "victor" is Arab disunity... and what premise has been proven exactly? That Arabs are stubborn? That unity of antagonists is impossible? (And, if so, impossible in general, or just impossible for Lawrence to pull off?)

THREE SCREENPLAY STRUCTURAL SYSTEMS. Three insufficiently resolved explanations of *Lawrence's* structure. We could go on analyzing this film forever; Robert McKee alone provides so many potential diagnostic categories, I wouldn't even know where to begin. It's clear, though, that by any yardstick, you can't accuse *Lawrence of Arabia* of being a typical film. The story is strewn with conflicts, all of them basically incidental. The film really exists, or so it seems, to provide a framework for one maddeningly elusive question: *Who was this guy?* And it doesn't even answer it. It just asks it — over and over again, which may be why people have come back to this film for fifty years now. Maybe they're hoping that *this time*, the sands will shift in their favor, and the mysteries will finally be solved.

EXERCISE: *LAWRENCE OF ARABIA*

Despite its ample onscreen oppositions, *Lawrence of Arabia* is a film driven by elusive, hard-to-pin-down conflicts, resulting in a thematically ambiguous picture. Name two other films driven by ambiguous or obliquely defined themes. What are the central conflicts of these films, and how do the three acts bring these conflicts to a Point of No Return and resolve them, if they are indeed resolved (and if the films even have three acts to begin with)?

Film #1 _____

Number of Acts _____

Central Conflict _____

Conflict Definition _____

_____

_____

Point of No Return _____

_____

_____

Resolution _____

_____

_____

Film #2 _____

Number of Acts _____

Central Conflict _____

Conflict Definition _____

_____

Point of No Return _____

_____

Resolution _____

_____

_____

LOST HORIZON
(1937, 134 min.)

Screenplay by Robert Riskin
Based on the novel by James Hilton

SCREENWRITER ROBERT RISKIN and producer/director
Frank Capra are one of the most celebrated partnerships in motion picture history. Together, they created a number of beloved
films, including two Best Picture Oscar winners, *It Happened
One Night* and *You Can't Take It With You*. The "Capriskin"
team was also responsible for *Lost Horizon*, which is likewise
frequently deemed a "classic," though not on merit alone. In
fact, *Lost Horizon* provides a clear-cut example of a "good" film
that doesn't work, and vividly illustrates how the collapse of a
screenplay's dramatic conflict can ruin an otherwise well-made
movie based on an interesting idea.

Most of my script analyses here have been primarily centered on structural issues. But because the problems with *Lost
Horizon* run deeper than just a question of act breaks, I will be
relying more directly on the breakdown template I provided on
page 82, and we'll be digging much deeper into character here
than we have with any of the films we've discussed so far. The
extra effort will be worth it to determine precisely where the
problems with this film lie.

Analysis: Structure

Are there three acts? Act One of *Lost Horizon* kicks off with
British diplomat Robert Conway in China, hustling a group of
Anglo tourists and dignitaries onto a plane to escape a Chinese
rebellion. They fly to the Himalayas, where their pilot loses his
way and is forced to land in the mountains. The travelers are
met by a strange band of locals who offer to take them to shelter.
Act One ends with Conway and the refugees arriving in Shangri-
La, a grand mountain sanctuary city that they soon discover has

magical properties (thirty-four minutes into the film; 25% of the running time).

Act Two covers the refugees' idyll in Shangri-La, and how they are all (well, *almost* all) transformed by its sorcery. Shangri-La is a world of perpetual peace where no one ever gets sick, dark thoughts and fighting are a distant memory, and people live to staggeringly old ages with their youthful beauty intact. Chronically ill socialite Gloria Stone recovers her health, Yankee hustler Henry Barnard builds plumbing for the mountain city, and fussy geologist Alexander Lovett finds happiness teaching science to Shangri-La's children. Conway is perhaps the most profoundly touched, first by Sondra, a Shangri-La resident with whom he falls in love, and then by the High Lama, the great holy man of this utopian outpost. The Lama shares his vision of Shangri-La with Conway, a vision of a place where the world will gather when it tires of war, ignorance, and destruction, a place where all earthly knowledge will be collected and truth and beauty will reign forever.* It's a seductive vision, and Conway believes he has found where he truly belongs.

Though it seems to the travelers that they only spend a few weeks in Shangri-La, several years actually go by. Time slows to a crawl in this place. Unfortunately, as you may have gathered, so does the story. Conflict, as we've well established, is the essence of drama, so how do you build dramatic tension in a land with no conflict? For a solid hour of screen time, basically nothing happens — except the realization of how dull it is to watch people just having a good time.

The only member of Conway's traveling party who doesn't fall under Shangri-La's spell is his brother George, who can only think of getting back to "civilization." George, too, has fallen in love in Shangri-La, with Maria, a beautiful "young" Austrian girl

---

* A large portion of the High Lama scenes was among the seven minutes of film footage that had been lost by the time the American Film Institute initiated the restoration of *Lost Horizon* completed in 1986. The audio for these scenes still exists, however, and is included in the DVD version of the film, illustrated with still photographs from the production.

whom he refuses to believe is really an octogenarian. Finally, tired of waiting for a promised rescue that never seems to be coming, George decides to leave Shangri-La, and as Act Two closes (116 minutes in; 87%), he manages to persuade Conway to abandon his own dreams (and Sondra) and come along with him.

Act Three consists almost entirely of Conway, George, and Maria wandering through the mountains, tormented by cold and rough travel. Maria starts aging rapidly, and soon, as a frail old woman, she dies of exposure. In his despair, George hurls himself to his death over a cliff. Forced to go on alone, Conway is soon rescued by a band of travelers from the "real" world, but all he can think of now is getting back to Shangri-La... never mind that he shouldn't have left in the first place. By the way, this last part is not seen onscreen, but *told* to us by the stuffy members of an English gentlemen's club. This scene is the only time we see these men in the entire movie; they seem to be in the story only to tie up the ending... and to break the "show, don't tell" rule, which is fundamental Screenwriting 101 stuff.

Who are the antagonists? Another reason *Lost Horizon* flounders is the lack of a solid antagonist. There are no invaders or marauders threatening Shangri-La's perfection. Conway and his fellow refugees may not share the same goals during their time in the mystical city, but no one is attempting to actively subvert anybody else. The closest we get to an antagonist here is George — and all he wants is to go home. This lack of antagonism keeps the story's conflict, and thus its drama, at a soporifically low ebb. After an exciting first act, the film grows excruciatingly dull.

What is the conflict? As indicated above, *Lost Horizon* is seriously wanting for conflict. The opposition between Conway and George, rather than driving the story, merely symbolizes the *real* conflict, which is an ideological one. This film is about the clash between who we are and whom we wish to be, between the real world and the idealized world of our dreams, here represented by Shangri-La. In other words, this film is *allegorical*, with characters who by necessity are flat, existing primarily to express philosophical points. Unfortunately, philosophical treatises do not often make for compelling drama, and *Lost Horizon* illustrates why, as it consistently subordinates character and dramatic conflict to its "message."

When is the conflict defined, and in what manner? Before it becomes the film's defining conflict, the reality/idealism dichotomy enters the story as an abstraction at the end of Act One. The world we have seen up to this point (the "real" world) is a place of tension and hostility, revolution and poverty, where good people try their best to maintain equilibrium in a world unraveling around them. This world contrasts with Shangri-La, where conflict is virtually nonexistent and all citizens are free to pursue their ideal selves. These worlds don't actively butt heads, but they are clearly on opposite sides of the coin. So there is, in fact, a real conflict here. Too bad nothing of a dramatic nature is done with it.

What is The Point of No Return? The Point of No Return arrives when George finally confronts Conway about the "illusion" of perfection with which Shangri-La has hypnotized him. At last, the abstract opposition between the real world and Shangri-La is out in the open, and Conway is presented with a choice: the potentially lethal certainties of reality, or happiness that may just be an illusion. He chooses reality and leaves Shangri-La with George. Better the flawed world that you know is real, he figures, than a perfection that may exist nowhere except in the imagination.

How is the conflict resolved? Once he leaves Shangri-La, Conway receives irrefutable proof that its perfection was real, as Maria turns into an old woman before his eyes, then perishes. He knows now that perfection *is* possible... and that he turned his back on it. He sacrifices everything and nearly kills himself in an arduous years-long trek through the mountains, but he finally makes it back to Shangri-La. Idealism triumphant. It's a typically utopian "Capriskin" ending, a finale suggesting that if we sacrifice and give ourselves over to our better natures, we too can achieve a state of bliss. It's a naïve view, but Capra's films are beloved the world over for comforting images like these. Indeed, given its lack of strong narrative conflict, *Lost Horizon* is ultimately more effective as utopian propaganda than as drama.

NOW I'M GOING TO ANALYZE CONWAY to illustrate how botched character construction is often part and parcel of a flawed conflict.

Character Analysis: *ROBERT CONWAY*

What does the character want? This very first question runs us right into another problem with *Lost Horizon*. Through most of the picture, we have no idea what, if anything, our main character is after. Early on, Conway seems perfectly content with the life of a diplomat. He knows that international politics is a win-some, lose-some business, but he's been toiling in its trenches for years. He seems to want nothing, so right off the bat, there's nowhere for him to go as a character. Later, in Shangri-La, he falls in love, realizes he's found utopia, and now has a concrete goal: to live out his (long) days in Shangri-La in perfect peace and happiness. Still, this realization doesn't occur until deep into Act Two; it's awfully late in the story for our protagonist to be finding a goal.

Another problem is that achieving this goal requires no risk, indeed no action at all, on Conway's part. All he has to do to make himself happy is stay put – and grind the story to a halt, which is why Riskin is forced to have George talk Conway into escaping. Never mind that abandoning Shangri-La runs directly counter to his achieving the only goal the script has established for him.

If Conway doesn't leave Shangri-La, he doesn't do anything, and the story will come to a dead stop. The behavioral logic of the character is sacrificed just to keep the story moving forward.

Are there obstacles in his path? As suggested above, not really. For the first half of the picture, Conway has no clear-cut goal, so whatever obstacles he encounters are not obstructing his movement toward anything specific. Even when Conway talks to the High Lama and realizes that he wants to share in the utopian ideal of Shangri-La, *still* no obstacles emerge, because he's already achieved what he just realized he wanted. He's already in Shangri-La, he's comfortable and happy, he loves Sondra and she loves him. It's the perfect world that all his diplomatic efforts, however noble, were unable to create. All he has to do is stay right where he is, and he's got what he wants, with no real obstacles to his bliss.

Of course, once Conway chooses to leave Shangri-La, his obstacles reach enormous proportions. A gigantic range of dangerous mountains and frigid, slashing weather hinder his return to the magical city. When he's finally rescued and shares his story, he's (not surprisingly) thrown into an asylum. He has to steal vehicles to attempt a return to Shangri-La, and he is constantly being locked up in sanitariums and prisons from which he is forced to escape. And, of course, once he evades the authorities, he still has to get *back* over the mountains to return to Shangri-La.*

These obstacles are daunting, to be sure. But it's hard to feel much sympathy for Conway, *whose goal had already been achieved*. If he'd just stayed in Shangri-La, he never would have had to deal with any of this mess. Successful stories have been written in which characters choose to enter a conflict, rather than being *forced* into one against their will. But this strategy is always launched with a clear-cut goal *that is still out of the character's reach*. Conway, on the other hand, has the brass ring

---

* More stuff we only hear about from our stiff-upper-lipped friends at the gentlemen's club.

firmly in hand... and throws it away just because his brother pitches a fit. It's almost a version of Roger Ebert's "Idiot Plot," where a film's entire story could be resolved in five minutes... if every character in the film weren't an idiot.

Do the obstacles force him to make choices? Well, Conway's happiness is only threatened once he makes the decision to leave Shangri-La with George... a bad decision, as it reverses his previous choice to stay and thus directly undermines the achievement of his greatest desire (a desire, I can't stress enough, that Conway had already achieved). So, once Conway goes back out into the mountains and loses his brother (the person who talked Conway into abandoning his dream in the first place), he becomes so desperate to reclaim his former joy that, despite the arduous journey facing him, he can only make one choice: get back to Shangri-La and re-embrace the magic *that he willingly walked away from for no good reason.*

In overcoming those obstacles, is his inner life revealed? Again, not really. By the time he realizes that Shangri-La is his dream come true, Conway essentially has no more inner life. He wears his feelings on his sleeve, and his desire for utopia is the only thing driving him. His reasons for leaving Shangri-La are vague, based more on misguided loyalty to his brother than anything else, and by the time he realizes he made a mistake, all inner conflicts, doubts, and neuroses melt away, leaving one clear, all-encompassing goal: get back to Shangri-La or die trying. The situation makes for a somewhat uninteresting protagonist, but this style of characterization is common in allegories, where characters exist primarily as mouthpieces for the writer's ideas and agenda.

Does he enter into conflict in Act One? As noted above, the primary conflict of *Lost Horizon* is an ideological one, reality versus illusion. Though this dichotomy doesn't actively affect Conway until the end of Act Two, the very fact that he's in

Shangri-La brings the opposition between reality and the ideal into his sphere of experience. One could therefore say that Conway enters into *Lost Horizon's* central conflict in Act One simply by traveling to Shangri-La in the first place. Still, at the time, he doesn't recognize this arrival as an initial confrontation with the film's conflict... nor do we.

Is he pressured to change in Act Two? Not until the very end of the act. In fact, rather than placing him in situations of tension and suspense, Shangri-La mellows Conway, transforming him into a romantic utopian. And he adopts this new personality willingly, like a dreamer sinking into a soft feather bed. No pressure required. Not until George tries to coax him into leaving Shangri-La is any kind of change *forced* on Conway. He is asked to turn his back on his joyous new life and re-enter "reality," no matter what it might cost him.

Does he change in Act Three? More like changes *back*. When Conway watches Maria age and die while they're lost in the mountains, an event that drives his brother to suicide, he realizes what a fool he was to leave, and his romantic idealism comes rushing back, overtaking him for a second time, for good (one assumes). After this occurrence, Conway can think of nothing but returning to Shangri-La, where utopians are the norm rather than curiosities.

———————

IT IS CLEAR THAT *LOST HORIZON* suffers from serious problems of structure and characterization. A film like this one, made by some of the most talented and celebrated filmmakers of the era, is a cautionary example to us. After all, arguably the most celebrated screenwriter in 1930s Hollywood dropped the ball here big time, and if we don't heed the lessons provided by films like this one, we may someday find our own work serving as a "what not to do" example in a book just like this one.

EXERCISE: *LOST HORIZON*

What would you, as a screenwriter, do to fix *Lost Horizon*'s essentially "broken" structure? How would you alter Act One to install a less abstract, more action-and-character-driven conflict as the story's engine? How would this conflict build in Act Two, and what would be its Point of No Return? How would the conflict be resolved to end the story? Briefly outline the conflict breakdown of your three-act structure below.

Act One Definition of Conflict _____

_____

_____

Act Two Conflict Buildup and Point of No Return _____

_____

_____

_____

_____

_____

Act Three Conflict Resolution _____

_____

_____

_____

_____

_____

PSYCHO
(1960, 109 min.)

Screenplay by Joseph Stefano
Based on the novel by Robert Bloch*

AS SOME OF YOU MAY HAVE ALREADY GUESSED
Psycho is the script I alluded to in several of the previous analyses. This screenplay is the rule breaker that works.

Employing a structural gambit that others have attempted to duplicate since, with usually nowhere near the same success, Alfred Hitchcock and his screenwriter, Joseph Stefano, blew the conventional shape of storytelling all to hell. Midway through the story, the protagonist – the point of audience identification, Our Heroine – gets splattered like a bug on a windshield. Then, the film attaches its focus to the only other character we've gotten to know... the killer! *And it works!* Confounding all expectations, *Psycho* leads us by the nose to a jolt of adrenaline-fueled excitement, and years will pass before the viewer can shower with equanimity again.

So, let's see how this script that shouldn't work works.

Analysis: Characters and Situation

Who are the characters? Troubled, alienated Eisenhower-era Americans trying (and mostly failing) to make themselves happy. Specifically, they are Marion Crane, a bank secretary whose desperate act of larceny sends her on a collision course with a nightmarish destiny; Marion's fiancé, Sam, and sister Lila; hard-nosed detective Arbogast; and Norman Bates, the backward, socially awkward desk man at an isolated motel overlooked by a house he shares with his monstrous, domineering mother – or so we think.

---

*An unacknowledged source for *Psycho* is William Faulkner's tale "A Rose for Emily" (1930). Although the plots are not identical, it is impossible to walk through Mrs. Bates bedroom, with the impression of her body etched so deeply into the mattress, without thinking of Miss Emily.

What are the conflicts?

Conflict #1: GOOD MARION VERSUS "BAD" MARION. Marion Crane suffers a crisis of conscience after she steals $40,000 from the bank where she works. She freezes when she sees her boss as she's driving out of town. She's suspicious of everyone who tries to talk to her after she's taken the money and haunted by an accusing cacophony of voices in her head that follows her all the way to the Bates Motel. Ultimately, Marion settles this inner crisis, but she meets a brutal end before she can affect the result of this resolution. Issue: *Will Marion do the "right" thing?*

Conflict #2: SAM, LILA, AND ARBOGAST VERSUS NORMAN. The external conflicts among characters in this film center mostly around Norman Bates. He's desperate to conceal his mother's crimes from the world, while Sam, Lila, and Arbogast, suspecting him (rightly) of involvement in Marion's disappearance, will do whatever it takes to catch him in a lie. Issue: *Will Norman help his mother get away with murder, or will Sam, Lila, and Arbogast expose Mrs. Bates' crimes?*

Conflict #3: A COUNTRY IN CRISIS. As in *King Lear*, the characters in *Psycho* are at the mercy of a fundamentally flawed universe. Decent, hardworking folks are unable to catch a break (both Marion and Norman, in their own ways, are victims of economic circumstance), the honest life is without rewards, mothers are monsters when they should be nurturers. And, of course, through both Marion and Norman, the film suggests that people are never truly what they seem, that deep within us all lurks a criminal impulse. *Psycho* tells us that anyone, if pushed hard enough, is capable of anything; however, this conflict is less an "active" one in the film than an environmental one, contributing to an unsettling *mise-en-scène* that enables the film's bloody goings-on.

Conflict #4: NORMAN VERSUS "MRS. BATES." This conflict is the film's central one — a powerful internal struggle that torments Norman and, ultimately, drives him to murder. The callow, sensitive Norman is caught in a battle for control of his mind against "Mother," his broken psyche's manifestation of the woman who so heartlessly dominated him in life that even killing her didn't end her draconian control over him. Mother's personality is so vividly drawn by Hitchcock and Stefano that we sometimes have to remind ourselves* that this conflict exists entirely within Norman's fractured mind, rather than between two separate characters. Issue: *Which personality will finally win control of Norman Bates?*

When is the conflict defined, and in what manner? *Psycho's* first act, which culminates in the establishment of the Norman-versus-Mother conflict, is a structural gamble more daring than any of the film's numerous visual and stylistic tricks. Stefano's script provides *Psycho* with what has come to be known as a "false first act," setting us up to follow the story of Marion Crane's flight from the law, and then, in the shower at the Bates Motel, pulling the rubber no-slip flowers right out from under us.

This first act uses every conceivable trick to deceive us into thinking that we are *not* watching a story about a mentally deranged killer; Norman, whose internal conflict and resultant murders drive *Psycho*, doesn't even appear onscreen until nearly a half-hour into the film. Instead, we first meet Marion and learn of her troubled love for the divorced Sam and of the financial woes keeping the pair from marrying. (Conflict #3 is in full swing from the first scene, and remains so through the entire film; the characters are in a constant struggle against the dictates of this flawed universe and, just like in *Lear*, they never gain the upper hand.) We follow Marion as she robs her employer and leaves town, kicking Conflict #1 into high gear (fourteen minutes into

---

* That is, if we already know what's coming when we watch the film, which few first-time audiences did back in 1960.

the film, 13% of the running time). We are completely invested in her as she is confronted by suspicious strangers along the way, and we hear the imagined voices of her loved ones and coworkers tormenting her with guilt. All of our interest and emotion is invested in Marion and the hole she's dug for herself, and we have been thoroughly tricked into believing she is the film's main character as she pulls into the Bates Motel, twenty-six minutes in (24%).

Enter Norman – an immediately intriguing character. We listen, along with Marion, as Norman argues bitterly with "Mother," and we feel for him as much as we have for Marion as he discusses his lonely life, his difficult relationship with his mentally ill mother, and his futile desire for escape.* We momentarily wonder if these two troubled yet attractive people might become involved. We even assume Norman's voyeuristic point of view as he spies on Marion through a peephole. Still, as compelling as Norman may be, he wasn't even in the film's first thirty minutes, so all our instincts as film viewers, and our subconscious knowledge of the rules that almost all films follow, tell us that Marion must be *Psycho's* protagonist. But observant viewers may have noticed something amiss right from the opening credits, where Anthony Perkins is given top billing and Janet Leigh (Marion), the film's biggest star and, thus far, the actor with the most screen time, is listed last.

Nevertheless, nothing up to this point has indicated that this film is about anything but Marion Crane, her theft, and her escape. Robert Bloch's original novel introduces Norman and Mother before we meet Marion, so in the book there is already a sense that Norman is possibly the real main character of this story. Hitchcock and Stefano were bolder, making us believe that Norman is just an interesting detour on Marion's journey... a journey that looks as if it's about to come to a swifter-than-anticipated end when Marion, brooding alone in her room at

---

*Norman's dialogue, as written by Stefano and spoken by Anthony Perkins, is outstanding in its expressive awkwardness. No rulebook can ever teach you how to write like that.

STRUCTURAL ANALYSES 157

the Bates Motel, makes the decision to return the money and face the music. Conflict #1 resolved: The good side of Marion's personality wins out.

Then, forty-seven minutes into the film (43%), our illusions about Marion's primary position in the story are upended, along with traditional story structure, as Mother pulls aside Marion's shower curtain and slashes the helpless woman into bloody rags. In the postmodern era, when films like *Pulp Fiction* and *Memento* routinely play structural games, recalling what an audacious departure *Psycho* represented in 1960 is difficult. People raised on formula Hollywood storytelling watched in shock as a lunatic with a butcher knife killed a film's "main character" less than halfway through the picture. Everything they understood about the rules of cinematic storytelling died in that shower with Marion. Hitchcock almost loses us when he kills her off, but within minutes he has managed, in his genius, to recapture our interest as we watch Norman — the only other character in the film with whom we have been invited to sympathize — being forced to deal with the consequences of his mother's bloody crime. And so, *Psycho's* real central conflict, the lethal relationship between Norman and Mother, comes to the fore.*

What is The Point of No Return? To focus our rattled attention after Marion's murder, Hitchcock and Stefano immediately foreground the investigation of Marion's disappearance. Sam and Marion's sister Lila are hunting for her, and Arbogast is on the case as well, hired by her boss to find the missing money. But before the detective can uncover the secrets, Mrs. Bates dispatches him to detective heaven. This is the second of the film's two on-screen murders and, although it seems like an obvious Point

---

* It's a hell of a writing achievement, to be sure, but one of the reasons this story works is surely the presence of Anthony Perkins, who was typecast for life by this portrayal but who said, in later interviews, that the part was so good he took it despite knowing how it would hamstring his career choices. It would not seem a promising character with whom to be permanently identified, and yet people have great affection for Norman — as they often do for victims, which is what he is at the core. The lesson for the screenwriter: If you're going to kill off a Janet Leigh, be sure you have a Tony Perkins waiting to take the spotlight.

of No Return at a natural point in the story for such an event (seventy-seven minutes in; 71%), it is not. After all, we already know at this point that Mrs. Bates is a murderer, so killing the detective doesn't change our understanding of her or of Norman, and it doesn't really raise the stakes of Conflict #2. What are they gonna do — put Mrs. Bates in the gas chamber twice?

Not until Sam and Lila visit the local sheriff after Arbogast's murder do we learn that circumstances in the Bates house are even stranger than they seem. Mrs. Bates, the lawman informs them, has been dead for ten years, following a rather unpleasant crime that is only alluded to. Sam doesn't understand; he's sure he saw an old woman in the window of the house above the motel. "Well, if that woman up there is Mrs. Bates," the sheriff asks, "who's that buried out in Green Lawn Cemetery?" (eighty-four minutes in; 77%). The characters now know that something is deeply wrong at the Bates house, which seals their determination to get to the bottom of the mystery at all costs. This resolve neatly brings both Conflicts #2 and #4 to a simultaneous Point of No Return, as Sam and Lila move into their final confrontation with Marion's killer, just as we realize the depth of the horror overwhelming Norman Bates.

How are the conflicts resolved? Back out at the Bates Motel, Sam distracts Norman while Lila goes up to the house to snoop around. We are given a privileged view of Mrs. Bates' plush Victorian-style boudoir — a stark contrast to Norman's sad little hovel of a room. It's like a trip to the two warring halves of Norman's mind; these rooms already hint at the personality struggle going on in the house, and to its ultimate resolution. Finally, Lila comes face to face with Mrs. Bates' hideously preserved corpse in the fruit cellar... and "Mother" bursts in on them, wielding a knife. It's Norman in old-lady drag, and the inhuman, high-pitched cry that escapes from "her" lips makes it brutally clear that nothing is left of Norman. The film's central conflict, between Norman's two personas, has been decided: Mrs. Bates has obliterated her beleaguered son.

———◆———

PSYCHO CONCLUDES WITH A LENGTHY SCENE in which a psychiatrist explains the nature of Norman's dementia, his mother's crimes, and how her personality came to overtake his own. In a way, this scene is largely unnecessary. Those two bedrooms and the stricken rictus of Norman's face as his wig falls to the floor tell us everything we need to know about the horror that's gone on in that house. Still, it's nice to have this closing scene to depressurize us and bring us back to earth. After the jolt of the final confrontation, consider this scene your long sigh of relief.

EXERCISE: *PSYCHO*

Psycho is famous for its daring use of a "false first act," lulling us into thinking the film is about one subject, then pulling the narrative rug out from under us at the first-act curtain. Can you think of any other examples of films with false first acts? Choose two, one in which this bait-and-switch structure works, and one in which the film falls apart. Discuss the nature of their false first acts, the reversals that occur at the first-act curtain, and why this gambit works for your first film, whereas your second falls flat on its narrative face.

Film #1 _____

False-First-Act Story _____

_____

_____

First-Act Curtain Reversal _____

_____

_____

Why it Works _____

_____

_____

Film # 2 _____

False-First-Act Story _____

_____

_____

First-Act Curtain Reversal _____

_____

_____

Why it Fails _____

_____

_____

SOME LIKE IT HOT
(1959, 121 min.)

Screenplay by Billy Wilder and I. A. L. Diamond
Based on the German film *Fanfaren der Liebe*,
written by Robert Thoeren and Michael Logan

COMEDY IS A RELENTLESSLY DIFFICULT storytelling form to analyze because its inherently subversive nature makes playing fast and loose with rules almost a matter of course. Plot and structure often take a back seat to the jokes, the perception being that if the film makes you laugh, it's done its job, even if the story's not up to snuff. Comedy is almost the only genre in which a haphazardly structured or even plotless film can still work, as long as the jokes are funny enough.*

Still, some comedies score huge laughs while telling a structurally sound story. So it is with the legendary *Some Like It Hot*, the American Film Institute's choice for the funniest comedy of all time. In fact, as much of the humor in this film derives from funny performances and good jokes as it does

---

* As my analysis of *Dumb & Dumber* makes clear, your mileage may vary regarding this point.

from a slick narrative structure that sets up laughs and beautifully pays them off.

Analysis: Characters and Situation

Who are the characters? Jerry and Joe (soon to be "Daphne" and "Josephine"), two Depression-era jazz musicians on the run from gangsters; an all-girl jazz band fronted by the gorgeous Sugar Kane; and various gangsters, show folk, and tippling old millionaires.

What are the conflicts? *Some Like It Hot* is driven by several conflicts, two primarily external and relationship-driven, one an internal conflict within one of our central characters.

> Conflict #1: JERRY AND JOE VERSUS THE GANG-STERS. This pairing is the film's most overtly antagonistic conflict, the one that gets the entire narrative ball rolling. Chicago jazzmen Jerry and Joe unwittingly witness the St. Valentine's Day Massacre (carried out in this film not by Al Capone but by fictional mobster "Spats" Colombo) and are forced to go on the run to avoid getting rubbed out themselves. Their flight from Spats gets the boys into drag (they take jobs as the bassist and sax player for an all-girl band heading to a hotel gig in faraway Miami), and this initiates everything else that happens in the story: Joe's romance with Sugar, Jerry-as-Daphne's dalliance with drunken millionaire Osgood, and so on. *Some Like It Hot* is primarily a romantic farce, but without the hoodlums in the first act, Joe and Jerry would never get all dressed up, let alone have a place to go. Issue: *Jerry and Joe's necks, and how to save them.*

> Conflict #2: HOW TO MARRY A MILLIONAIRE. Once the "girls" get down to Miami, the story orbits around the attempts of several characters to land, or to present themselves as, potential rich husbands, an enterprise fraught

with complications and proliferating ironies on all sides. Sugar, whose self-destructive weakness for musicians (especially saxophone players like the besotted Joe) motivates her instead to seek the romantic company of a shy, bespectacled millionaire, drives Joe to steal yachting clothes and pass himself off as filthy-rich petroleum scion "Shell Oil Jr." in an attempt to win Sugar's heart. Meanwhile, "Daphne," roped unwillingly into a date with Osgood, finds himself torn when the old rummy proposes, offering him the life of financial security he's always craved... but at some price. The core obstacle facing these connections, naturally, is the deceit being perpetrated by one of the lovers. Joe's no millionaire, and of course "Daphne" is no lady. Issue: *The battle of the sexes... whatever they may be.*

Conflict #3: JOE VERSUS JOE. In addition to the acrobatic plot complications, *Some Like It Hot* boasts a solid internal conflict in the character of Joe. When we first meet him he's your garden-variety louse with women, prone to manipulating and sweet-talking them for his own ends. But then, when he's forced to masquerade as a typical victim of his own sleazy behavior, he gets an up-close look at how the other half lives, thinks, and feels. Joe's internal struggle is cranked up when, as "Josephine," he's forced to act as romantic counsel to Sugar, who's planning her conquest of "Shell Oil Jr.," never suspecting that he and her new best girlfriend are one and the same. Issue: *Joe's status as a heel, and its potential impact on his relationship with Sugar.*

When are the conflicts defined, and in what manner? *Some Like It Hot* opens with a police raid on a Spats Colombo speakeasy, where Jerry and Joe are working as musicians. Out of a job, thanks to the cops, the two buddies stop by the office of a well-known theatrical agent, but find that the only work currently available for a bassist and sax player is in an all-girl band heading to play a Miami hotel. Jerry's willing to consider going into drag for the gig, but Joe shoots down the idea in disgust, illustrating his issues with women, which drive Conflict #3. But this conflict is in full swing right from the get-go, in the way Joe ogles the speakeasy's dancers and in how he manipulates the agent's secretary, Nellie, with promises of romance (he's already stood her up for a date once, before the story begins), only to turn it into a request to borrow her car for an out-of-town gig. Simply put, when it comes to women, Joe is not "a bit of terrific." He's a bum — but his lesson is coming soon enough.

The boys go to a local garage to pick up Nellie's car… and walk right into the St. Valentine's Day Massacre. They escape with nothing worse than a few bullet holes blown in Jerry's bass, but Conflict #1 has started with a literal bang (twenty-three minutes into the film; 19% of the running time). Their old boss is now after their heads and things look bad… until Joe gets a bright idea, calls up the agent, and asks, in a high-pitched "girlie" voice, if the all-girl band gig is still available. The next time we see Jerry and Joe, they're tottering down a train-station platform in full drag, on their way to Miami as "Josephine" and "Daphne." (Jerry was supposed to be "Geraldine," but changes the name at the last minute. In general, Jerry takes to being a woman much more easily than the chauvinistic Joe. Indeed, Jack Lemmon stays almost exclusively in drag for the rest of the picture).

As the "girls" get underway with Sweet Sue and her Society Syncopators, they get to know their fellow bandmates, especially Sugar Kane (née Sugar Kovalchik), the ditsy-but-sweet lead singer. During a secret late-night drinking party on the train, Sugar tells "Josephine" all about the troubles with men that have kept her on the run from band to band. She has a weakness for saxophone-playing louses like Joe, and hopes that in Miami she'll find a shy, quiet millionaire who will really love her and take care of her for life. Though Joe's inner conflict has already been established (forty-four minutes into the film; 36% of the running time) when Joe learns what one of his dalliances is like from "the fuzzy end of the lollipop," this conversation marks the moment he starts to realize he will have to confront these harsh truths about himself. It also establishes Conflict #2, the girls' search for sweet, rich husbands: Sugar's quest to land a millionaire is mirrored, in Shakespearean low-comedy style, by Daphne's relationship with filthy-rich old drunk Osgood Fielding III. They meet at the hotel in Miami when he helps Daphne with her lost high-heeled shoe, tickling her ankle and pinching her in the elevator (fifty minutes in; 41%).

What is The Point of No Return? As the girls play their gig in Miami, various romantic subplots start tangling up the story. Joe, who has swiped some yachting clothes from the band's road manager, disguises himself as Shell Oil Jr. and strikes up a liaison with Sugar. The girl singer is in seventh heaven, never suspecting that this guy is a total sham. He's not rich; he doesn't own a yacht (Joe smuggles Osgood off of his own yacht, for a date with Daphne, so he can use it for the night); he's not impotent like he claims to be just to get Sugar to kiss him... he doesn't even need the glasses he sports.* As Conflict #2 deepens, Conflict #3 seems to be regressing; Joe's falling back into his familiar patterns, lying to Sugar and toying with her affections. But this behavior isn't like the previous times. Joe's really falling for this woman... and because, in disguise as Josephine, he hears Sugar's private thoughts and feelings about the relationship, something else is happening that never has before: He's seeing one of his potential conquests as an honest-to-goodness person. Meanwhile, Jerry's date with Osgood has reaped its own unexpected rewards. The old lush has proposed to Daphne, and he's said yes, figuring that he can spill the truth to Osgood after the "I do's" and get himself a nice fat settlement check. The stakes on Conflict #2 have risen to the boiling point; both Jerry and Joe are now in a position in which they're

---

* He also doesn't talk like Cary Grant... though the voice Tony Curtis puts on certainly makes everything he says as Shell Oil a lot funnier.

eventually going to have to put up or shut up regarding the deceptive nature of their relationships.

But wait a minute — wasn't this movie supposed to be about two guys on the run from gangsters? *Some Like It Hot* is quite daring in terms of structure, using the freedoms allowed by the comedy genre to its narrative advantage. Once Jerry and Joe's initial conflict with the gangsters has been established, the antagonists are removed from the film for the entire middle hour, and the life-or-death tension of the crime plot dissipates as Jerry and Joe conduct their romantic dalliances. For a while, it seems as if the boys have gotten away with their ruse, escaping not only with their lives, but also maybe with some dough (for Jerry) and true love (for Joe).

But just past the ninety-minute mark (*Some Like It Hot* runs a hair over two hours, unusual for a comedy at that time, but more common today), when everything seems well on its way to the sunny shores of Happy Ending Land, the film takes a dynamite twist when the all-but-forgotten Spats arrives at the hotel with his thugs for a mob conference. Spotting the gangsters, Jerry and Joe realize the jig is up. Their time as Daphne and Josephine has run its course, and it's life-or-death stakes again as we reach The Point of No Return.

How are the conflicts resolved? As the boys prepare to flee the hotel, Joe calls Sugar and, posing as Shell Oil Jr., tells her he's leaving the country on oil company business… namely an arranged marriage to a South American oil heiress. Sugar's heartbroken, but so is Joe, who now knows how it feels to be on the fuzzy end of his lollipop. Back in drag, the boys are ready to make tracks when Josephine hears the band playing in the hotel lounge; Sugar's onstage, singing the saddest version of "I'm Through With Love" you've ever heard. Conflict #3 is resolved in daring fashion as Joe, who now knows exactly how a woman really feels, steps onstage and kisses Sugar full on the lips, telling her not to cry: "No guy is worth it." (That he's in full drag when he kisses her gives the moment a gutsy charge.)

Then it's back on the run and, as they bring Conflict #1 to its resolution, here's the one place in the story where Billy Wilder and his cowriter, I. A. L. Diamond, fudge things a bit. Jerry and Joe hide under a table in the hotel's banquet hall, finding themselves trapped as the gangsters gather for their meeting. There, Wilder and Diamond introduce Little Bonaparte, a vindictive old gang boss who chews out Spats for his handling of the garage massacre. He then has a giant birthday cake wheeled out for Spats... never mind that it's not his birthday for months. Out of the cake pops a hitman who tommy-guns Spats and his crew. In the confusion, Jerry and Joe escape from the banquet hall with gunmen still on their heels. If they can just get to the docks and Osgood's yacht (he's been called to aid in the escape and is waiting for Daphne), Conflict #1 will finally be settled.

Little Bonaparte, frankly, is kind of a cheat. We hear nothing about him until he shows up in Act Three, and he is clearly in the picture only to get Jerry and Joe off the hook with Spats. In short, he's a classic *deus ex machina*, something screenwriters are taught to avoid. He takes the conflict's resolution out of the protagonists' hands and makes it contrived and arbitrary; still, Wilder and Diamond have otherwise done their job so well — and made us laugh so much — that we're willing to forgive this storytelling shortfall in a way we wouldn't if this were a straight-up crime thriller. Besides, we're much more invested in the romantic plot than in the business with the gangsters, and the writers do not let us down in tying up the ends of this aspect of the story. Jerry and Joe make it to Osgood's waiting shuttle craft, where they are joined at the last minute by Sugar. Joe admits everything, telling her she should run away from him as fast as she can. The education of a heel is complete, and he's finally put a woman's well-being ahead of his own gratification; of course, she'll have none of it, and falls ecstatically into Joe's arms. Conflict #2 is resolved for Sugar; she's got her millionaire... even though he's not one. Jerry, meanwhile, tries desperately to convince Osgood of the myriad reasons why they can't marry.

Osgood brushes off every last one, until Jerry finally rips off his wig and confronts him with the undeniably masculine truth. And Osgood... well, he takes the news better than you or I probably would. Conflict #2 is resolved for Daphne. She's got *her* millionaire... too bad she's not Daphne.

———————

THOUGH OBVIOUSLY A FILM not without its little (Bonaparte) flaws, *Some Like It Hot* holds up better than many Hollywood comedies of any era. And if Wilder and Diamond bobble the ball a little in bringing their story to a close in suitably hilarious fashion, well...

Nobody's perfect.

EXERCISE: SOME LIKE IT HOT

Some Like It Hot takes a storytelling gamble by placing the resolution of one of its main conflicts in the hands of a *deus ex machina*. Name two other films in which a *deus ex machina* resolves a conflict: one in which this resolution works, and one in which the result is narratively unsatisfying. Outline the use of the *deus ex machinas* below, and why their usage works and fails in their respective films.

Film #1 _____

Deus ex Machina _____

_____

_____

How it Resolves the Conflict _____

_____

_____

Why it Works _____

_____

_____

Film #2 _____

Deus ex Machina _____

_____

_____

How it Resolves the Conflict _____

_____

_____

Why it Fails _____

_____

_____

———————

SO, WHAT HAVE THESE ANALYSES PROVEN?

We have illustrated that the principles of dynamic structure work across a broad range of film styles and genres, and that they have been in place throughout the history of cinema. In fact, these principles proved to be effective *before* cinema, as Shakespeare's *King Lear* and Ibsen's *A Doll's House* also conform to these structural dictates. *Crouching Tiger, Hidden Dragon* shows that these narrative ideas do not work simply for Western storytelling, that they can apply to stories from other nations and cultures as well. We've seen what happens when a story fumbles its approach to both conflict and character (*Lost Horizon*), and we've shown that a screenplay can play fast and loose with the rules of structure, provided the writer really knows what he's doing (*Psycho*). We've outlined, with *Invasion of the Body Snatchers*, a structural system based around escalating moments of tension, which we will discuss again in much more specific detail in Chapter Ten. We've shown that a satisfying cinematic experience can be brought out of a screenplay that seems, on its surface, a tangled web of ambiguous characters and conflicts (*Lawrence of Arabia*). And, with *Dumb & Dumber*, we've even proven, as if some of the major box office hits of the last twenty years weren't proof enough, that sometimes an audience will make a hit out of a film with a structural disaster of a screenplay.

These are all micro-lessons stemming from the main lessons of these analyses:

(1) Dynamic structure works as a system for structuring screenplays.

(2) This system is not written in stone. You can break the rules and still create something great. But...

(3) You really better know your stuff first. As they say, you have to know the rules before you can break them effectively.

(4) Following the rules is not the same as being uncreative. All the films we analyzed here that conform to dynamic structure do so in different and interesting ways. And there's no reason that your script can't be different and interesting, too.

Chapter Eight

DO-IT-YOURSELF SCRIPT ANALYSIS,
or Take YOUR Word For It!

*I want to know my whole story works
before I start writing.*

— Tom Schulman

———————

WHAT FOLLOWS IS AN OPPORTUNITY to apply the principles of script analysis discussed in the last chapter to screenplays of your own choice. Feel free to copy the following pages and use them for dynamic-structural analyses of any scripts you like. I would actually suggest throwing a few badly structured scripts into the mix as well. You can't really know that something works, after all, unless you've likewise seen how something *doesn't* work.

I also advise you to plug a few of your own screenplays into this formula. For beginning and intermediate writers, this exercise may be a valuable tool in analyzing your work for potential weaknesses, whereas more advanced writers will find the exercise useful for confirming that you've done your job well... or discovering that you haven't and didn't realize it. (Hey, if it can happen to Robert Riskin...)

EXERCISE:
APPLYING DYNAMIC STRUCTURE TO STORY

Screenplay Title _____

_____

Screenplay Genre _____

_____

Who are the characters? _____

_____

_____

What are the conflicts?
Conflict #1 _____

_____

Conflict #2 _____

_____

Conflict #3 _____

_____

Conflict #4 _____

_____

When are the conflicts defined, and in what manner?
*Conflict #1*_____

_____

_____

*Conflict #2*_____

_____

_____

Conflict #3 _____

_____

_____

Conflict #4 _____

_____

_____

_____

What is The Point of No Return?
*Conflict #1*_____

_____

_____

*Conflict #2*_____

_____

_____

Conflict #3 _____

_____

_____

Conflict #4 _____

_____

_____

How are the conflicts resolved?
Conflict #1 _____

_____

_____

Conflict #2 _____

_____

_____

Conflict #3 _____

_____

_____

Conflict #4 _____

_____

_____

EXERCISE:
APPLYING DYNAMIC STRUCTURE TO CHARACTER

What does the hero want? _____
_____
_____
_____

Are there obstacles in his/her path? _____
_____
_____
_____

In overcoming those obstacles, is any of his/her inner life revealed?
_____
_____
_____

Does he/she enter into conflict in Act One? _____
_____
_____
_____

Is he/she pressured to change in Act Two? _____
_____
_____
_____

Does he/she change in Act Three? _____
_____
_____
_____

Chapter Nine

STORY TYPOLOGY,
or It's in the Way that You Use It

People just want to watch movies that are entertaining;
it doesn't matter what genre it is.

— Matthew Vaughn

———

THERE ARE SEVERAL *TYPES* OF STORY. And when I say *type* here, I don't mean *genre* — a label that usually has more to do with the story's external trappings than with its emotional or narrative effect on the viewer. For example, if a film features gunfights, horses, and ten-gallon hats, it's a good bet you're dealing with a Western. But what *type* of Western? *The Wild Bunch* and *Blazing Saddles* both more or less fall into the Western genre, but I don't think even a casual viewer could confuse the two. Type is more about what the story *does* with the genre it's chosen, the narrative points it makes through its characters and themes.

Here are four common story types:

Drama

In broad terms, *drama* means "a story about conflict." Narrowly, it refers to a type of story, regardless of genre, in which the author attempts to impart a *new truth* about the human condition. In the old days, human psychology was studied not in a laboratory, but through the novel and theater. Ian Rodger calls novelists "unpaid sociologists who make up for their lack of statistical evidence with inspired guesses."[23] Because of the

---

[23] Robert S. Paul, *Whatever Happened to Sherlock Holmes? Detective Fiction, Popular Theology, and Society* (Carbondale: Southern Illinois University Press, 1991), 6.

drama's dual requirements of novelty and truthful expression, writing a good one is not easy. Most fall short and become…

Melodrama

Basically, poor man's drama. "Melodramatic" is generally synonymous with "lurid," and "melodrama" with a story bloated with plot contrivances. The purpose of melodrama, writes Pauline Kael, "is primarily to entertain (by excitation) rather than to instruct."[24] Melodramas may impart truths, but they are shopworn truths, otherwise known as *clichés*. Soap operas, for example, are melodramas trading largely in narrative cliché.

According to Anthony Burgess, melodramatic plots are "dependent on coincidence or improbability."[25] But these useful contrivances are not the privileged domain of melodrama alone; some of the greatest, most revered plots in all of fiction hinge on moments of improbable coincidence. More often than Burgess and other scholars may care to admit, a carefully chosen improbability does the best job of creating a situation extreme enough to allow "high drama" to exercise its powers of revelation. One of your goals as a writer is always to put your characters in a situation that will draw out behavior that is normally never seen. Take *Oedipus Rex*: A man kills his father *without realizing it's his father*, then marries his mother *but doesn't know it's his mother*. Look at *Who's Afraid of Virginia Woolf?* When things get truly crazy and terrifying during dinner at George and Martha's house, at no time do Nick and Honey simply get off their duffs and leave, as almost any sane person would. These stories and many others manage these improbabilities by creating the narrative motif of "*What if?*" What if Nick and Honey stayed? What if Oedipus committed these atrocities without knowing he was destroying his own family? The key, what separates melodrama from "high drama," is that great dramatists choose

---

[24] Pauline Kael, I *Lost It at the Movies: Film Writings 1954 to 1965* (New York: Marion Boyars, 2007), 324.

[25] From Burgess' essay on "The Novel"; bibliographical citation on p. 75 of this book.

their implausibilities with purpose and care. Hacks just litter them all over the place, thus, Kael writes again, "In contrast with drama, which sensitizes man to human complexity, melodrama desensitizes men."[26]

Tragedy

A *tragedy* is a specific kind of drama in which a character is brought low by his or her own human frailty, a character trait that has commonly come to be known as the *tragic flaw*. In classic tragedy from Sophocles to Shakespeare, the tragic hero is a "noble" person, whether by reasons of wealth, birth, glory, or simple virtuous character. But as Arthur Miller shows in *Death of a Salesman* – generally regarded as the greatest modern tragedy – high station is not an essential aspect of the tragic character. A common man like Willy Loman can also be a tragic hero; or, perhaps Miller's work shows that, where dreams and desires are concerned, there are no common men. In any case, don't forget that your tragic screenplay can just as easily be about a cabdriver as about a king.

Jack Miles writes:

> The classic Greek tragedies are all versions of the same tragedy. All present the human condition as a contest between the personal and the impersonal with the impersonal inevitably victorious.* If any one of the circumstances that lead so inexorably to the downfall of Oedipus in Sophocles' *Oedipus Rex* had been different — if as an infant he had been abandoned on another road than the one he was actually abandoned on; if Jocasta, his mother, had died before his return to Thebes; if any link in the chain had been broken — then his will to know the truth, his "tragic flaw," would not have been his ruin. But it was foreordained that events should proceed through this and only this course and that his end should

---

[26] Kael, 327.

* Given this definition, one could possibly cite *Moby-Dick* as the definitive American classical tragedy. It's hard to think of an adversary more impersonal, or more definitively victorious, than Melville's great white whale. (Footnote courtesy of the author of this volume.)

therefore be ineluctably what it is. The spectacle is cathartic to the extent that it succeeds in suggesting that all human lives are variations of the collision it presents. Sophocles invites us, by grieving for Oedipus, to grieve for ourselves.

Hamlet is another kind of tragedy. Though we see Hamlet in a set of circumstances that involve, just as those of *Oedipus Rex*, veiled and revealed truth and a tangled, passionate relationship among the protagonist and his parents, the tragic outcome never seems inevitable. Moreover, Hamlet's flaw, endlessly debated, is located somehow in his character and so would remain a flaw in any of a variety of other circumstances. The particularity of the set of circumstances in which we see him does not play the role the comparable set plays in Greek tragedy. The contest is unlike that between doomed, noble Oedipus and an iron chain of events. It is, instead, a conflict within Hamlet's own character between "the native hue of resolution" and "the pale cast of thought."[27]

Arthur Miller himself offers the following observation: "I think the tragic feeling is invoked in us when we are in the presence of a character who is ready to lay down his life, if need be, to secure one thing — his sense of personal dignity." Tragedy, then, "is the stuff of those doomed few who say no and are willing to pay for saying no."[28]

And pay they do, for all tragic heroes end up the same way: annihilated. And not just physically, either. Something tells me that Oedipus would gladly stay blind if it meant he could take back the misdeeds that led him to that condition. "The tragic pattern," adds Leland Ryken, Professor of English at Wheaton College, "consists of six elements that are remarkably constant: dilemma — choice — catastrophe — suffering — perception — death."[29]

---

[27] Jack Miles, *God: A Biography* (New York: Vintage, 1996), 397–398.

[28] Victor Davis Hanson and John Heath, *Who Killed Homer? The Demise of Classical Education and the Recovery of Greek Wisdom* (New York: The Free Press, 1998), 271.

[29] Leland Ryken, Ph.D., "The Bible as Literature," in *The Origin of the Bible*, ed. Philip Wesley Comfort (Carol Stream, IL: Tyndale House, 2004), 130.

Tragedy is generally regarded as the highest form of drama. The most "serious" authors always write stories with unhappy endings, and they are considered the most serious because they write the truth — namely, that all life is tragic because all life ends badly. Everybody dies. Thus, all happy endings, by their nature, are incomplete endings, because they are *not really the end*. Any happy ending is manufactured by stopping the story short, breaking it off at a joyous moment. The dawn before the darkness, so to speak.

Comedy

In *comedy*, we are invited to view the characters' sufferings *from the outside*; that is, we are detached from the characters and do not feel their pain, which renders their struggles ridiculous. This detachment from the characters' troubles distinguishes comedy from other story types in which we are invited to view the characters' difficulties from within, and thus to share their perspectives, including their pain. No less an authority than Mark Twain said, "The secret source of humor itself is not joy but sorrow. There is no humor in heaven."[30]

Laughter is a burst of ecstatic pleasure whose function is *apotropaic*; that is, it serves to avert or ward off evil. *Laughter negates fear.* By laughing, we defang a threat. (Think of the seemingly inappropriate laughter you'll hear from the audience during some of the most gruesome moments in horror films.) Humor, it follows, is often about terrible things; the subject of comedy is frequently *that which frightens us*. Being attacked is frightening, but *impotent attacks* are funny. Being taken by surprise provokes a jolt of fear, but as soon as we regain our composure, we laugh. Therefore, *surprise* is an important element of comedy (and helps explain why most jokes are seldom as funny the second time you hear them). *Meaninglessness* is

---

[30] Mark Twain, from *Pudd'n Head Wilson's New Calendar.* Quoted in *The Bible According to Mark Twain: Irreverent Writings on Eden, Heaven and the Flood by America's Master Satirist*, ed. Howard G. Baetzhold and Joseph B. McCullough (New York: Simon and Schuster, 1996), 373.

also threatening; therefore, nonsense and incongruity are funny, as long as they fail to overwhelm us. In the words of Immanuel Kant, "Laughter is an effect that arises if a tense expectation is transformed into nothing."[31]

Drama places us, by identification, in harm's way. We allow the characters inside our own skin, or we enter theirs, and their discomfort becomes ours. But comedy removes us to a safe distance, fortifying us with what Henri Bergson called "a momentary anesthesia of the heart."[32] Or, as Will Rogers said, "Everything is funny as long as it is happening to someone else."

It may interest you to know that both Franz Kafka and Samuel Beckett considered themselves humorists. To the rest of us, their writings are alternately terrifying and depressing. But their work operates at the extreme level of the fear they were attempting to neutralize; unable to escape their own dread, they thrust it at arm's length by rendering it absurd. That the comic nature of Kafka and Beckett's work does not register for most of us as comic demonstrates that if it is to connect with its audience, comedy must match that audience's own fear level. Persons with mild, unthreatened lives require a commensurate humor. If your worst fear is an unruly lawn, you will laugh when Fred Flintstone mows his grass with a lizard.

---

[31] Immanuel Kant, *The Critique of Judgment* (New York: Oxford University Press, 2007), 161.

[32] Henri Bergson, "Laughter: An Essay on the Meaning of Comic," in *Comedy*, ed. Wylie Sypher (New York: Doubleday Anchor, 1956), 63.

EXERCISE: STORY TYPOLOGY

This chapter has identified and explained four common story types. Choose two films and, in the spaces below, state whether the films you have selected would typically be considered drama, melodrama, tragedy, or comedy. Provide examples of story events, character behavior, or aspects of narrative structure that lead you to classify these films under the story type designations you have selected.

*Film #1*_____

_____

Story Type _____

_____

What Makes it This Type? _____

_____

_____

*Film #2*_____

_____

Story Type _____

_____

What Makes it This Type? _____

_____

_____

Chapter Ten

ON PACE, EXPOSITION, AND TWISTS, *or Introducing Hedonic Adaptation*

Unless man can make new and original adaptations to his environment as rapidly as his science can change the environment, our culture will perish.

— Carl Ransom Rogers

On Pace

DYNAMIC MOVEMENT IS THE ESSENTIAL ELEMENT of effective storytelling. Each scene should naturally lead into and propel the next. Recall Aristotle's words: "It makes a great deal of difference whether the incidents happen because of what has preceded or merely *after* it."

Fiction writing instructors frequently advise that you keep preplanning of any writing project to a minimum. The idea is that you should just sit down in front of a blank piece of paper or computer screen, start writing, and see where it leads. When you write this way, conventional wisdom has it, each scene tends to naturally suggest the next. *Let your characters guide their own destinies*, they say. *Don't manipulate them like puppets*. The problem with this method of writing (except in those exceedingly rare cases when the gods toss you their thunder) is that eventually you run out of steam, and your narrative grinds to a dead halt, usually late in the second act, at a place where you really don't want to be. (By which I mean a place that cannot take you anywhere at all narratively speaking and is by itself in no way a satisfactory finishing point for your story. It's like running out of money in Benson, Arizona.*) At that point, it's a great deal of trouble to salvage your story without simply throwing out most of what you've written, which is a massive exercise in frustration, enough to make most of us abandon the thing altogether.

Planning out your scenes and fitting them into a structural model has the virtue of making sure you never end up dead in the water like that. On the other hand, though, it presents the disadvantage that when you sit down to write, your presketched scenes have this awful tendency to end without "suggesting" the next scene on your list. Narrative flow is continually being disrupted, and you have to work like a dog to rewrite each scene so it does suggest the next. It's not enough to just have good scenes. Each scene must also push into the next one (unless, of course, your goal is to constantly be providing your audience with places in the story where they feel like they can run to the bathroom). This keeps your story's pace trucking along and your audience right on board with your characters.

Still, both methods of story development have their own difficulties, which is just a way of saying that there's no way in screenwriting to avoid a lot of work... that is, if a good screen-play is your goal. If you don't care, well, it's still a lot of work. And that's why I hate writing a bad script; it takes just as much work as writing a good one.

On Exposition

> *The tragedies of Aeschylus and Sophocles used the subtlest devices to furnish the spectator, in the early scenes (and as if by chance), with all the necessary information. They showed an admirable skill in disguising the necessary structural features, and making them seem accidental.*
>
> — Friedrich Nietzsche

---

* And if you've ever been to Benson, you know what I'm talking about.

It's hard to find a better description than Nietzsche's for the concept of *exposition*. Basically, that means background information – facts the audience needs in order to comprehend the world of your script or the relationships of your characters, but that you can't think of any way to communicate except by putting them directly in your characters' mouths (even though they would presumably possess much of this information already). Exposition is notoriously difficult to write, and much of it sounds terrible, sticking out from the rest of a film's dialogue like a plug ear. Exchanges like: "Have I told you that, since you're my eldest son, and our family runs the canvas industry in Schenectady, and the gross national product of Urdustan is burlap, here we are in downtown Mandragore risking everything to corner the versatile jute market?" "Yes, but I can never hear it enough."

I've never liked cramming a lot of supposedly "necessary" information into a limited space, especially at the beginning of a film. In the case of *Alien*, the awkward exposition I was dealing with concerned the spacecraft's mission. I didn't want the craft to be a typical military or quasi-military spaceship, like on *Star Trek*; that was too familiar to audiences and would allow them to dismiss the film as "just science fiction." To shock viewers into a sense of "reality," I wanted to show them something they hadn't seen before: a *used future*. I imagined a kind of tramp-steamer look for the ship, so I decided these guys were prospectors who had bought a secondhand ship and gone to the center of the galaxy to mine for rare ores. But when I started writing, I couldn't find a natural-sounding way to explain this to the audience. I just kept having the characters talk about mining, and every time it came out clumsy: "Well, here we are back from mining the asteroids. Aren't you happy we bought our own ship so we don't have to split the profits?" Ugh. Real people don't say things like that; we're not constantly "reminding" each other who we are and the context of what we're all doing. And that was my problem. The characters weren't saying this stuff to each other. They were saying it to the audience, and it sounded phony, because it was.

After struggling with this dilemma for far too long, I started wondering if the audience even *had* to know any of this. Have you noticed how when you come into a movie late, you rarely have a tough time picking up on what's happening? You may not know the setup, but you can certainly follow the action from one minute to the next. If I came into *Star Wars* a half-hour late, I would miss some good scenes, but following what I did see wouldn't be a problem. I mean, it's basically guys rocketing around in spaceships, having adventures. Eventually you'll put two and two together, and in the meantime your ignorance really doesn't interfere with your enjoyment of the bit you *are* watching.* So I decided that *Alien* itself would "come in late": If some of my exposition was unnatural or contrived in the presentation, then it must have been inessential to the storytelling. If it sounded unnatural to say it, then the audience didn't need to know it. Who cared if the crew were miners, or Marines, or intergalactic pea-pickers? *This movie wasn't about mining*; it was about people on a spaceship fighting an alien, so that was all the audience *needed* to know.

I eventually figured out that audiences supply their own explanations for missing information anyway, and it's usually just as good as — or better than — what the filmmakers already had in mind. Tell an audience too much and it gets bored, because you're spoon-feeding it. Tell the viewers not quite enough, on the other hand, and they'll become alert and start guessing and supplying answers to their own questions. They'll become engaged, which is always the most enjoyable way to watch a movie.

Thus, a rule of thumb for exposition: *If the audience doesn't need to know it in order to follow the immediate story, get rid of it!*

---

* When I was a kid, it wasn't unusual for people to arrive at the theater halfway through a movie, sit through the second half, wait out the intermission, then sit through the first half and leave!

This advice is not intended to suggest that all dialogue should be subject to this utilitarian treatment. Characters obviously need to share information in order to move a story forward. But there is a difference between characters telling things *to each other* and telling them *to the audience*. Only the latter should be eliminated because the resulting dialogue sounds completely unnatural.

On Twists

Twists have been toying with the expectations of the audience since the beginning of dramatic storytelling. In the *Poetics*, Aristotle called them "reversals," but regardless of what word one uses, they are simply narrative revelations that change both the characters' and audience's understanding of the preceding events, and of the potential events and outcomes to follow. In *Oedipus Rex*, the big twist comes when Oedipus discovers that he has murdered his father and married his mother. In another classic (and equally incestuous) twist, *Chinatown* hinges on the moment when Faye Dunaway's character reveals that the mysterious young lady everyone's looking for is her sister *and* her daughter. The master of the story twist was Alfred Hitchcock, whose films are rife with narrative rug-pullers such as dead characters who aren't really dead (and "living" characters who are really stone dead, the most famous being, of course, Mrs. Bates in *Psycho*).

Lemme tell you how to write a good twist: You begin by leading the audience to believe that something terrible is going to happen — not just anything, a creeping unknown — but a *very specific* terrible thing. As the story develops, everything further convinces the audience that this exact terrible thing is going to happen. Audience expectations build to the breaking point, and the viewers brace for the moment when the terrible thing happens. All logic tells them – insists unambiguously – that precisely *this* terrible thing is going to happen, and no possible other.

Then, finally, a terrible thing indeed happens – but it's a *completely different* terrible thing from what the audience expected. Not only that, but it's much worse than what it had predicted... and *even more logical* than anything it had anticipated. What you want is your entire audience shouting as one: "*Oh my God! Of course!*"

A great example of this astonishment occurs in *Seven*, written by Andrew Kevin Walker. Remember how they catch the seven-deadly-sins killer in that movie? *They don't.* Everything leading to the film's third act drives us to believe that, no matter how diabolical and brilliant the killer seems, it's only a matter of time before the heroes nail him. They've gotten so close, after all, and so often. But then, at the second-act curtain, what happens? The killer turns himself in. *And it's all part of his plan*, setting up a third act that ends with the killer triumphant — and Gwyneth Paltrow's head in a box.

The Phony Terrible Thing is a red herring *par excellence*. All of your efforts must go into deceiving the audience, keeping it from suspecting what the *real* terrible thing will be. Like a stage magician drawing his audience's attention away from the rabbit in his back pocket, you must sweep it under the rug, use every trick of distraction in the book. Of course, if the audience second-guesses you and figures out the *real* terrible thing in advance, the entire effect is ruined. But if you've done your job well, when the *real* terrible thing happens, it will come as a staggering revelation. All of the audience's preparation, everything it has done to steel itself for the impact of the *phony* terrible thing, is blown away by the nuclear blast of the truth: The worst horror is worse than anything they could imagine... and it's so logical that they should have seen it coming. But now it's too late.

And so you have written a good twist, and everyone will love you. Audiences were so thrilled by the twist ending of *The Sixth Sense* that M. Night Shyamalan has built an entire career on its impact. Each film he's made since then has met with harsher reviews and less enthusiastic audiences, so much so that many have asked how he's still even able to make movies. The answer: Everyone's hoping he's got one more masterful Phony Terrible Thing hidden up his sleeve.

———————

PACE, EXPOSITION, AND THE CLEVER DEPLOY-MENT OF TWISTS are daunting obstacles in the creation of a screenplay. Fortunately, I've discovered a concept from the world of science that, while not designed for screenplays, nevertheless addresses all of these facets of script construction elegantly and well.

Hedonic Adaptation

In their 1971 essay "Hedonic Relativism and Planning a Good Society,"[33] psychologists Philip Brickman and Donald Campbell outline a concept known as *hedonic adaptation.* This concept is a physical and emotional reaction whereby people adapt to extreme change, or to any prolonged situation (pleasant or harmful), through a *dulling-down* of the situation's effects on the subjects experiencing it. As Brickman and Campbell explain, humans possess a surprisingly swift ability to adapt to change in their circumstances — an innate skill that allows them to maintain emotional equilibrium over time. Even exceptionally intense or traumatic situations, if sustained for a significant enough period, will lose their unfamiliarity and eventually come to be perceived as "normal."

As a real-world example of how this process works, consider gasoline prices. A few years ago, when gas first hit the then-unprecedented price of three dollars a gallon, tremendous public outcry ensued. Now, we'd be thrilled to find ourselves paying "only" three bucks a gallon, and further upward swings

---

[33] Published in *Adaptation Level Theory: A Symposium*, ed. M. H. Appley (New York: Academic Press, 1971), 287–302.

in gas prices have not seemed nearly as traumatic as that first three-dollar peak.

For another example of hedonic adaptation, look no further than sexual response, or more specifically, the concept of the multiple orgasm. If your partner has already climaxed once, only a fool would continue to focus his stimulation efforts on the same "key" areas. The appropriate tactic here would be to back off and tend to less prominent erogenous zones, or to spots that are generally considered unrelated to sexual response (the toes, the back of the knee, perhaps a nip or two to the neck), keeping your partner tantalized while giving him or her some relief from the most intense sorts of stimulation. Then, once his or her level of arousal has been eased to an appropriate degree, but not tamped down entirely, you can again hit the "main drag" and ramp the action up to another successful climax.

I believe that hedonic adaptation's effects are especially strong with regard to visual stimulation. When critics and audiences speak about a film really "drawing them in," this phrase is just a way of saying that the experience of viewing the film in question is so intense that it essentially alters the circumstances of the audience's lives for the duration of the viewing. A film, when it's working, basically becomes the present "life situation" of its audience. This appeal makes the pacing of a film, its ebb and flow of action, information and narrative reversals, central to its effectiveness. Especially in a genre like action or horror, which depends on fairly direct means of audience stimulation (the adrenaline rush of an action scene, the heart-racing reaction to a monster's attack), an improperly paced film, without appropriate rests and pauses to allow impactful moments to have their full effect, will, over time, dull the audience's response to each of those impacts.

Like the lover discussed above, you, the writer, are basically seducing your audience. The viewers have willingly entered the theater and given their emotional lives over to you for the duration of the film. In your screenplay, the impact of each of your story points or twists will be much greater if the audience is given an appropriate amount of "down-time" following a moment of revelation or shock. This suggestion is not to say that the story should pause in its forward momentum entirely; indeed, these "down" moments are usually the best place for you to include some necessary exposition. After all, the circumstances of the story experience have just changed, for both the characters and the audience, and they need to be brought up to speed on this new threat or problem you have just thrown at them. After being hit with a narrative jolt, your audience will be in a high state of alertness and quite attentive, so exposition fits in here very naturally without boring your viewers. Think of how many horror films, after the monster's first attack, have a "What the hell was that?" moment where the characters come to grips with the terror now threatening them and attempt to learn something about its nature and motives. Ideally, this sort of exposition should answer not just your characters' questions, but also the audience's. If you're doing your job properly, this expositional pause will only last long enough for the characters and audience to become accustomed to the new, elevated reality of their situation. Then... *boom!* You hit them with another twist, provoking new questions and carrying the audience to the next plateau of heightened experience and attention.

Of course, we have already discussed in detail a film that utilizes this exact kind of structure: *Invasion of the Body Snatchers*, which is built around a series of "revelatory shocks" that serve at regular intervals to elevate the tension and action within the narrative. These "shocks" are really narrative twists, altering the film's reality and heightening its terror every time they occur. Ideally, in your own writing, these jolts should hit the audience with ever-greater frequency as the narrative drives relentlessly forward.

A chart of the hedonic adaptation effect, as it applies to screenplay structure, might look something like this:

Hedonic Adaptation Effect

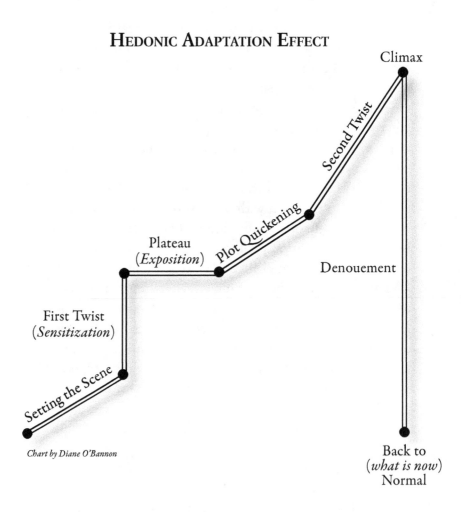

Chart by Diane O'Bannon

I've only included two twists for the sake of example, but your screenplay will probably need to include more. Ideally, each twist you include will be of greater intensity than the one before.

In short, thanks to hedonic adaptation, what an audience at first finds frightening and unexpected will eventually become "normal" to it within the context of the film. Hedonic adaptation is an involuntary physical response that cannot be controlled by the viewer; its effects shouldn't be ignored by the screenwriter, but rather used to his advantage. The key is to keep bringing the unexpected, amping up the intensity, raising the action to new heights. Any relaxation an audience experiences prior to the denouement should be temporary, if not entirely illusory – and, no matter what, your story should avoid taking us back to the "normal" world we encountered at the beginning. In a way, though, it really can't do that; after all, even if the monster is defeated in the end, we now know that the evil is out there… and who knows when we'll encounter it again?

EXERCISE: ON PACE, EXPOSITION, AND TWISTS

Many films use the twist-exposition-twist principles of structure outlined in this chapter to avoid the dulling effect of hedonic adaptation on the viewer. Select two films and, in the spaces below, note the twists that elevate the narrative to a new plateau of tension and suspense, as well as the minute at which each twist occurs in the film. Study your results to see if the twists come with greater frequency as the pace of the action heightens toward the end of the film, and note the nature and duration of the exposition passages following the twist.

*Film #1*_____

Twist # 1 _____

When it Occurs _____

Subsequent Exposition _____

Twist # 2 _____

When it Occurs _____

Subsequent Exposition _____

Twist # 3 _____

_____

When it Occurs _____

_____

Subsequent Exposition _____

_____

Twist # 4 _____

_____

When it Occurs _____

_____

Subsequent Exposition _____

_____

Twist # 5 _____

_____

When it Occurs _____

_____

Subsequent Exposition _____

_____

Film #2 _____

_____

Twist # 1 _____

_____

When it Occurs _____

_____

Subsequent Exposition _____

_____

Twist # 2 _____

_____

When it Occurs _____

_____

Subsequent Exposition _____

_____

Twist # 3 _____

_____

When it Occurs _____

_____

Subsequent Exposition _____

_____

Twist # 4 _____

_____

When it Occurs _____

_____

Subsequent Exposition _____

_____

Twist # 5 _____

_____

When it Occurs _____

_____

Subsequent Exposition _____

_____

Chapter Eleven

WHY THREE ACTS?
or Pass Ergo, Collect $200

*Life is a moderately good play with a
badly written third act.*

— Truman Capote

———————◆———————

EVERYBODY USES THE THREE-ACT STRUCTURE. At this point, it's practically a given. But why?

Now I can't prove what I'm about to say here, and it's hard enough to put into words even without the burden of proof. All I can tell you is that it seems, to my intuition, to be true.

To begin with, because I write feature-length theatrical movies, I generally do not work with a one- or two-act structure. I prefer a completely developed story — a full meal. One- and two-act stories are short-form and, because a form *beyond* two acts exists, I go for the max.

But is three acts really the max? Why not write a *four*-act story? Go for the *mega* max?

Well, look at it this way: You define your conflict; that's one act.

Then you escalate that conflict to a point of irreversibility; that's the second act. And the conflict *must* escalate; to merely reiterate it is just spinning your wheels. That's why I felt obligated, in the first place, to find a way to raise the conflict to a qualitatively higher level. The previous section on hedonic adaptation should explain why this trajectory is crucial.

So you've squeezed two acts out of this thing now and, in the process, set yourself up for a third act in which your conflict will be resolved. But what if you wanted to try and wedge *another act* between The Point of No Return and the last act? Why shouldn't you? (This concept is the hardest part of the idea to express in language, so please bear with me).

To begin with, I have never found a way, within this extra act, to escalate the conflict to another level. Maybe somebody out there can think of a way — once The Point of No Return has been established — to escalate the conflict further. But even if they could, I don't think your average viewers could sustain another escalation. You've excited them once by initiating a conflict, then surprised them with twists leading to The Point of No Return. But now *your element of surprise is used up!* The audience is burnt out on twists, so even if you managed to boost the conflict to even greater heights, your viewers would see it coming. You've already hit what should have been the conflict's ultimate escalation point once. The audience knows it can be done and, as soon as it can predict your storytelling moves, *you can't use those moves anymore.* In short, by the end of the second act, you should have used every variation you can wring out of your conflict. You've anted once, upped your bet once, and now it's time to call (and hopefully not fold). That is why I write three acts.

———————————

SOME PEOPLE BELIEVE that you should put the high point of your story right smack in the middle. But by the midpoint of the story, the audience members are starting to weary a little. They've been sitting on their butts for an hour, so if you hit your high point at the halfway mark, they've got another hour to go with nothing as exciting at that moment awaiting them. That is going to make the second half of the film seem much longer than the first... endless... eternal. By the time the audience reaches the high point of the film, its time sense is collapsing, so the film's pace should accelerate. Ergo, what follows the high point should be shorter than what you've just sat through. Ergo, the high point of your story should be *past* the middle. Ideally, it should occur around the film's two-thirds point, and probably not any later than three-quarters of the way through.

I have also heard something to the effect that a film's three acts should be equal in length, that is, forty minutes each. (I've alternately heard that the second act should be roughly half the length of the film, or basically the middle hour). This pacing seems to imply that audiences have some kind of device in their laps capable of detecting when an act ends, and also of translating elapsed time into estimated script page count. I imagine some hypothetical audience looking down at its act-length supercomputers, seeing a readout saying "ACT ONE ENDED: ONLY 28 MINUTES ELAPSED!", and an angry mutter (*"Cheat! Cheat!"*) billowing through the outraged, re-fund-demanding crowd.

True elapsed screen time is impossible for an audience to judge. *Objective time* means nothing on screen; *subjective time* is all, and it does not correspond to actual measurable minutes. In 1949, the late Robert Wise directed a film called *The Set-Up*, which told the story of an over-the-hill prizefighter, played by Robert Ryan, who is supposed to throw a fight but refuses. Wise used this film to carry out an "experiment in time" – film time, real time, and above all, *audience time* – which he spoke about at USC and, years later, discussed with me when I interviewed him for this book. He told me:

> We decided that it would be an interesting thing if we could tell this film in real time, that is, the actual length of time it would take if it happened… It was about a boxing match, and the whole thing was supposed to take place, from beginning to end, in a little more than an hour. And that's where we got the idea of putting clocks in the film, at the beginning, middle and end… I was trying to see if I could, using the clock, tell the film in the time it took to act it out…

It seemed to come out that way, that it took the same time on screen as the internal time of the story.

When they were finished, Wise found that the film, title sequence aside, ran an hour and eleven minutes. Clocks are referenced throughout the film: A big street clock shows us the time at the beginning (9:05), and again at the end (10:16). One hour and eleven minutes have transpired within the story, and that's also the running time of the film. If you had a clock next to you throughout your viewing, it would always match the clocks in the film. The result?

"It ended up not making any difference in the perception of the audience," Wise said. "There could have been any time in the world on those clocks; nobody would have known the difference. They could have been jumping back and forth all over the place for all the audience knew."

I can think of no reason why the acts of a film should be the same length, or even seem to be the same length. Whom does this symmetry please? What difference does it make? Who cares? I put as much information into each act as I need to make my point, and if the first act ends up taking half the film's running time to play out, then so what? The length of each act should be determined *internally*, by whether it holds the audience's attention and says everything it needs to say. Who are you making the film for, anyway? The audience, or the God of Proportionate Acts?

The fact is that people (including filmmakers) are always more comfortable with rules. It's terrifying to feel like you're flying blind, and having a bunch of rules creates the comforting illusion that you do, in fact, know your ass from a hole in the ground. But if the rules are wrong, *you're no better off than if you had no rules at all.* And what's worse? Without rules, you are forced to rely on intuition. With the *wrong* rules, however, you will override every intuition. Even the correct ones.

You may say, okay, but what *harm* will it do if all the acts are the same length? Plenty. The myth of Procrustes' Bed should tell you that you will likely end up either padding out the acts with dross to get them up to the "right" length, or yanking out good stuff to cut them down to size. And in the interest of what? Having an even forty pages? I can just hear the word of mouth now: "Hortense! You have got to see this movie! *The acts are all exactly the same length!*"

EXERCISE: WHY THREE ACTS?
Because you've all been such good boys and girls, for this chapter, I'm gonna give you an easy one. Select three films and break them down into a three-act structure, identifying the first- and second-act breaks and when they happen. Also, determine the "high point" of each film and note the minute within the running time where that moment occurs.

*Film #1*_____

_____

First-Act Break _____

_____

Second-Act Break _____

_____

High Point _____

_____

When it Occurs _____

_____

_____

*Film #2*_____

First-Act Break _____

_____

Second-Act Break _____

_____

High Point _____

_____

When it Occurs _____

_____

_____

*Film #3*_____

_____

First-Act Break _____

_____

Second-Act Break _____

_____

High Point _____

_____

When it Occurs _____

_____

_____

Chapter Twelve

LENGTH OF A SCREENPLAY,
or Filling the Digital Doggy Bag

A wonderful bird is the pelican
His bill will hold more than his belican
He can take in his beak
Food enough for a week
But I'm damned if I see how the helican.

— Dixon Lanier Merritt

SOMEBODY ONCE ASKED ABRAHAM LINCOLN how long a man's legs should be; he answered, "Long enough to reach the ground." Conventional wisdom says that because one script page equals roughly a minute of screen time, and most feature films run about two hours — 120 minutes — a feature screenplay should thus ideally be around 120 pages in length.*

This rule of thumb — one page equals one minute — arose from the desire to conform films to a prescribed length, partly because of the presumption that audiences' attention spans won't last much beyond two hours, largely because of exhibitors' need to schedule as many screenings per day of a film as possible. So if you're going to make a two-hour film, you'd need to know how long a script for a film of that length would be. This formula has become very important to the screenwriting world at large. But it has a serious flaw; namely, it's basically invalid.

In my experience, there is no genuine meaningful correlation between a screenplay's page count and the film's running time.

---

* Lately screenwriting gurus have altered that estimation to 110 pages, but 120 was what I first learned, and it's what I'm sticking with. Pluto's still a planet, too, for that matter.

The length of a finished film is entirely determined by the *pace at which it is directed*.

When John Carpenter and I made *Dark Star*, one of the scenes I wrote consisted of a single speech, delivered into the camera:

                    MISSION CONTROLLER

```
Hi, guys. Glad we got your message. You'll
be interested to hear it was broadcast
live, all over Earth, in prime time. Got
good reviews in the trades. The time lag
on these messages is getting longer; we
gather from the ten-year delay that you
are approximately 18 parsecs away. Drop
us a line more often, okay? Sorry to hear
about the radiation leak on the ship,
and real sorry to hear about the death
of Commander Powell. There was a week of
mourning here on Earth. The flags were
at half mast. We're all behind you guys.
About your request for radiation shielding,
sorry to report, this request has
been denied. I hate to send bad news when
you guys are out there doing such a swell
job, but I think you'll take it in the
proper spirit. There have been some
cutbacks in Congress, and right now,
considering the distance, we just can't
afford to send a cargo shuttle out there
to you. But I know you guys'll make do.
Keep up the good work, men!
```

So how long do you imagine that little speech would play on screen? Use the "one page = one minute" formula. Well, I'll tell you how long it ran: eighty-seven seconds. That's *one minute and twenty-seven seconds* — long seconds — for a speech that runs just about a half a page.

I wrote the screenplay for *Alien* assuming the result would be a roughly two-hour movie, and the first draft was 112 pages long. But when the project was taken over by 20th Century-Fox, two of the producers, David Giler and Walter Hill, started rewriting it. The "final shooting script," the end result of their labors and mine, was over ten pages shorter than my original draft. I didn't see a practical need for these cuts, but I granted them their assumption that the edits would result in a more briskly paced film.

Over the course of shooting, all sorts of lines were cut, these edits incorporated into the "continuity script," which was amended on a continual basis. Then, after the editing process, I learned that another whole scene had been excised in the cutting room. This scene had actually been filmed, and it featured Ripley finding Dallas woven into a cocoon and euthanizing him. The scene had been removed, I was told, for reasons of pace; it was believed to be slowing down the film's climax.

So imagine my bemusement when the final running time of the completed *Alien*, after all that cutting and fussing... was 117 minutes. That's just three minutes shy of two hours — and, if you subscribe to the one-page-equals-one-minute theory, five minutes longer than a film based on my script *should* have run. All things considered, and given the editing that had been done, I thought the film seemed a wee smidge on the *long* side. If you took the script as it was on the day they wrapped shooting, and removed the cocoon scene, as in the final cut, you were looking at a script of only eighty-some pages. So, based on the standard line on page count, how does an eighty-odd-page script get you a film pushing two hours?

I found out how when I saw the finished product. *Alien* ran so long because Ridley Scott had directed it at a very deliberate pace. He lingered over atmospheric elements like the sets and drew out the suspense until it cracked the audience's teeth. And you shouldn't assume that Ridley Scott's style was the only way that script could have been directed. Staged at a brisker pace, the film could have come in easily ten or twenty minutes shorter — or even more — with exactly the same content.

Another example of this phenomenon (practically a laboratory demonstration of it) is Universal's original *Dracula* (see analysis on p. 104), which was simultaneously filmed in two versions, English and Spanish, both available in the film's seventy-fifth anniversary DVD set. Foreign-language dubbing had not yet been perfected in those days, so Universal just shot the film twice, on the same sets. The English crew would shoot during the day, then the Spanish crew came in when they finished and shot at night. Universal may have just wanted a throwaway picture for the Mexican market, but director George Melford obviously didn't see it that way. The result is a film many consider to be superior to Tod Browning's English-language version. It also happens to be 103 minutes long... *twenty-eight minutes longer* than the seventy-five-minute English version. And these two films were shot *from the same script* — one that had been translated into Spanish (by B. Fernandez Cue), to be sure, but that in itself shouldn't account for that great a difference in running time.

So what happened? Simple: Melford plays things out with greater deliberation and attention to detail than Browning. He makes sure his story points are clearly understood, and he uses more camera setups.* Which version is better? Honestly, that's neither here nor there. My point is not that one film is superior, but that this difference offers concrete proof that you can't gauge a film's running time just by looking at the page count of its script.

Now, dialogue. You might think a dialogue-heavy script will necessarily run long. All that talk will surely take forever, and besides, dialogue adds more lines to a script's length than action does. But that's not how it has to be. All you need to do is have your actors talk fast. If you want to see a director scramble

---

* As an interesting result, Renfield becomes a much more pivotal figure in the Spanish version, virtually the center of the movie.

at the speed of light over mountains of complex dialogue, just load up Ken Russell's *Altered States*. To see it done well, watch *His Girl Friday*. Or take a look at *Cast Away*, written by William Broyles, Jr. and directed by Robert Zemeckis. This film has virtually no dialogue for its entire middle hour; the script's central section is a vast swath of action description broken up by a line or two of dialogue every few pages. Page count: Ninety-two. Final running time: 143 minutes.

A film's running time is actually determined prior to production, based on the desires of the producer, director, and studio executives responsible for the project. Some movies are only meant to be ninety minutes long. But, if you try handing a ninety-page screenplay in to a studio, you will be informed, to your disgrace, that you have failed to deliver a *professional* screenplay – that you have *cheated* them. And any argument that they are asking you for an extra thirty pages just to throw on the floor will be fruitless.

When I was living in France, I was at first put off by the small portion sizes in restaurants. It never seemed like enough food to me. But after a few days of dining in Parisian eateries, I realized that the French had it right. Their portions were *exactly the right amount of food* for an adult to eat at one meal, and counter to my expectations, I always got up from the table full.

My ideas of how much should be on a plate had been conditioned by being American. Customarily, the quantity of food served in U.S. restaurants is monumental. It's what Americans expect, and it's what they get. No other nation has the custom of the "doggy bag," because no other nation's restaurants serve you so much food that you have to lug some of it home.

And that is why studios insist that writers give them a 120-page script for a ninety-minute film: *greed*. Unless they get more out of you than they can ever possibly use, they feel unsatisfied, because they have not taken advantage of you, as is their due. (Next time you watch a film's special edition DVD, think of the deleted scenes as sort of a digital doggy bag.)

An argument often advanced in favor of writing overlong scripts is that, inevitably, some scenes are going to come out poorly when the film is actually shot. Having a couple of extra scenes in your back pocket allows you to excise the bad footage and still make feature length.

However, I discovered when working as a director that once the script is broken down into shooting days and assembled into a schedule, the producer always tells me that it's too long, way over budget – we can't afford all those *shooting days!* – and instructs me to cut some scenes. Still too long! Cut more! Make it shorter! Shorter, please! *Shorter!* There's a scene in *Cool Hand Luke* where the cruel warden makes Paul Newman dig a hole, and then fill it back up again. After wrangling with producers over shooting schedules, I feel that I know, with moral certainty, where screenwriters Donn Pearce and Frank Pierson got the idea for that scene.

If you are genuinely concerned with how long your script will play on screen, I suggest having your director act out the entire script for you, in one marathon session, and timing them. If it's running long, make him do it faster. Not long enough (bloody unlikely), and *that* will be the time for you to start worrying about wrestling more pages out of the script.

EXERCISE: LENGTH OF A SCREENPLAY

Track down the screenplays for two of your favorite films. Check the script's page count against the film's final running time, and see if you can determine what created those differences. Choose a key scene from the film. How long does the scene play on the page compared to its length in the finished film? Do any major scenes appear in the film that are not in the script, or vice versa? If so, how does this affect the film's running time?

Film #1 and Running Time _____

_____

Screenplay Page Count _____
Key Scene Page Count _____
Key Scene Film Running Time _____
Script Scenes Not in Film _____

_____

_____

Film Scenes Not in Script _____

_____

_____

_____

Film #2 and Running Time _____

_____

Screenplay Page Count _____
Key Scene Page Count _____
Key Scene Film Running Time _____
Script Scenes Not in Film _____

_____

_____

Film Scenes Not in Script _____

_____

_____

_____

Chapter Thirteen

INSPIRATION VERSUS RULES,
or Calling the Script Cops

*Lope de Vega, that "wonder of nature," the most
prolific playwright of all time... wrote more than
fifteen hundred plays. In his comprehensive study
of dramatic theory and practice,* Writing Plays in
Our Time *(published in 1609 and written in verse),
he stated openly and bravely, after having
introduced all the "rules": "When I have to
write a play, I lock up the rules with six keys."*

— Howard & Mabley

I SPOKE A LITTLE IN CHAPTER ELEVEN about the constant struggle between a writer's openness to inspiration and his fidelity to the established "rules" of the form, but I feel that this subject is important enough to command a little additional discussion.

Producers, studio execs, development people, basically anyone in a position to give a writer orders, will almost invariably, almost inevitably beat them to death with the "rules" of writing. Sometimes, writers will even take those rules and use them to cut their own throats.

Why does a dog wag its tail? Because the dog is smarter. If the tail was smarter, it would wag the dog. And that's my basic advice about rules in writing: Don't confuse the tail with the dog. Rudyard Kipling said, "When your Daemon is in charge,* do not

---

* By "Daemon," he means your muse.

try to think consciously. Drift, wait, and obey."[34] Stephen King says, "Writing is at its best – always, always, always – when it is a kind of inspired play for the writer."[35]

Writing is all about inspiration; it must always take the lead. When the heat is on and the muse is in effect, if you are flush with inspiration and the writing just works, the rules become meaningless and unnecessary. You only need rules if and when the script *isn't* working.

You may find yourself with a good script in hand, then you or somebody else notices, upon examination, that it doesn't conform to some rule or another, and your alarm bells go off. To your eyes, the script worked just fine up until that moment. But now you've unearthed a *theoretical flaw*. So you get to work "fixing" the problem… and in so doing, utterly wreck the script. And you'll never figure out why the script doesn't seem to work at all now. How could it not? I mean, hell, *it follows the rules, doesn't it?!?!*

I assure you that your audience doesn't give a fat flying fig about the rules of writing. A person goes to the movies to be thrilled, aroused, engaged, tickled, *moved*. And that process cannot be generated or judged by any set of rules. As horrifying as it is to contemplate, the only accurate gauge of the ultimate quality of your work is your gut, your intuition as a human being. Either you like it, or you don't. And if you do, *don't mess with it*, even if it doesn't "obey the rules." If the script's working, no need to throw it under the microscope. Invoking the rules is like calling the cops: It's likely to get you into just as much trouble as it gets you out of.

My system of dynamic structure, as rules go, is actually pretty good. If your script has obviously run off the rails, it can put things back on track for you. To be crystal clear about this advice, my system can take a really stupid story idea and make it

---

[34] Rudyard Kipling, *Something of Myself: For My Friends Known and Unknown* (New York: Doubleday, Doran & Company, 1937), 210.

[35] Stephen King, *On Writing: A Memoir of the Craft* (New York: Scribner, 2000), 153.

sufficiently compelling that an audience can sit through it with minimal discomfort. If you know you're in trouble, that your story is structurally problematic, the system provides the means to get you out. But my system, or indeed any system, will never give birth to a great idea or spawn a brilliant piece of writing on its own. And there is nothing worse in the world* than watching some fool mangle a superb script in service of some idiotic rule.

Those who have ears, let them see.

EXERCISE: INSPIRATION VERSUS RULES

If you closely examine virtually any screenplay, including the established classics, you can probably spot theoretical flaws, ways in which that script violates the "rules" of screenwriting as preached by those in the know. Take two screenplays, preferably for films regarded as examples of quality writing, and identify a theoretical flaw. Explain why this fails to conform to the rules of screenwriting, and also why such a violation does not ultimately damage the script's quality.

*Script #1*_____
Theoretical Flaw _____

_____

How it Breaks the Rules _____

_____

Why it Doesn't Matter _____

_____

*Script #2*_____
Theoretical Flaw _____

_____

How it Breaks the Rules _____

_____

Why it Doesn't Matter _____

_____

---

* Next to fried eggplant, of course.

Chapter Fourteen

PERSPECTIVE,
or Phooey On What You Say

A little perspective, like a little humor, goes a long way.

— Allen Klein

————————————

ONE OF THE CHALLENGES facing every screenwriter, indeed every artist charged with making creative decisions, is how to view their own work with fresh eyes all the way through the lengthy creative process until the work is complete. This is *perspective*, and when you lose it, you've lost your most dependable means of judging your own material. Without perspective, who can tell if anything is bad or good? It all becomes a blur.

The problem is mental fatigue. For example, we all know what it's like trying to read a book when we're tired. Our eyes scan the pages, but our mind makes no sense of the words. A good night's sleep usually refreshes the reader and restores his ability to understand what he's reading. But for an artist embarked on a long project, the fatigue is specific to the work at hand, so one night's rest will not suffice. As William Goldman says, "You've thought about it so long, done it so often, in your head or on paper, that you start to get punchy, silly, dry."[36] The jaded writer needs to give himself enough time to *forget* his screenplay, so when he revisits it, the material seems as fresh and unfamiliar as if written by someone else. A night? In this case, a year might be more like it.

It is important to maintain a clear vision of your material in the beginning, when you still know it works. Make a kind

[36] William Goldman, *Marathon Man* (New York, Ballantine Books, 2001), xviii.

of rough mental representation of the work, and hang onto the memory of your feelings about your choice of good material when you were still fresh. At a later stage, when you no longer know what's right because your mind resembles a spin dryer, beware of the impulse to reconceptualize out of a sense of desperation or a dearth of new ideas. Consult your early decisions. Lean on them when you need to. Always remember your initial reactions to your material. They will be your best guide further down the road, when your ability to think clearly about your work has been worn down.

Producers and studio executives who have screenplays written on assignment are notorious for almost never being satisfied with the scripts they get. One reason for this response is that after watching the script being written and rewritten, draft after draft, they hit a saturation point with the material. For them, the script has gone sour, and they have no further capacity to like anything in it, because they greet its every line from a place of over-familiarity. Somebody else might like it at this point, though. Not necessarily someone any smarter than the producer or exec, but someone encountering the script with fresh eyes. But by this point, the wretched development producer simply moves from one disillusionment to the next.

To win arguments and intimidate you into submission, producers and directors will frequently use "loss of perspective" as a weapon against you. When explaining why they plan to ignore your soberest, most reasonable advice, and in an effort to neutralize the fact that you are more familiar with the script than they are (and might therefore have a deeper understanding of its problems), they will inform you, with smirking condescension, that you're too close to the material, you have no objectivity, your pride of authorship blinds you. You've lost your *perspective*. And that's if they assume you ever had any in the first place. But, explains the producer/director/studio executive, his or her own loftily disinterested perspective, so like an eagle's, is ideally qualified to make creative decisions about how best to vivisect *your* script.

But in the end, "perspective" is an empty argument, because nothing about producing or directing bestows upon one the least flicker of immunity to getting "too close/subjective/emotionally attached" to a movie one is fighting tooth-and-claw over. So don't get too demoralized by the "perspective" argument. All it means, when you boil it down, is "Phooey on what you say." And, if you honestly believe that your opinion is the right one in that situation, feel free to respond with "Phooey on your phooey."

EXERCISE: PERSPECTIVE
If you are able, find a copy of the first draft of a well-known screenplay, along with a copy of the film's final shooting script. Read both drafts and note differences between the writer's original vision and what finally ended up on screen. List these differences below, and discuss the ways in which these changes help, or hinder, the story being told.

Screenplay _____

Shooting Script Differences _____

_____

_____

_____

How They Help _____

_____

_____

_____

How They Hurt _____

_____

_____

_____

Chapter Fifteen

WHAT IS A PRODUCER?
or Not Who, What

*Producing is nothing more than bringing
all the elements together, connecting people.*

— Brion James

WHAT IS A PRODUCER? This question has troubled thoughtful persons for decades. To paraphrase Sir Arthur Conan Doyle, were they born that way, or does it come by degrees? On a less philosophical level, most people simply want to know: *What exactly does a producer do?* I mean, the producer is the one who walks away with the Best Picture award on Oscar night. There must be a good reason for that, right?

In his March 25, 1996 *Los Angeles Times* article "So You Want to Be a Producer," James Bates gave the best answer to this grand question that I have encountered in all my years of reading and considering the subject:

> Indeed, one of the more creative exercises in Hollywood is coming up with variations on the job title. Besides those already mentioned, there are line producers, executive producers, co-executive producers, supervising producers, coordinating producers, consulting producers, segment producers, and executives in charge of production.
>
> What do they all do? One of the problems with answering the question is that producing always has been a vaguely defined profession whose demands can range from working

12-hour days on location to simply knowing the right people. In its purest form, it can mean having the most influence over the shape of a movie: choosing writers, directors, actors and virtually everyone else associated with a movie.

The traditional definition is someone who acts as the chief executive officer of a picture, overseeing such areas as script development, hiring and casting, budgets, and problem-solving. The Producers Guild lists 26 functions, including determining the final shooting script, overseeing day-to-day operations, supervising music recording and even "the approval of makeup and hair styles." [Producer Lawrence] Turman has a simpler definition: "A producer is the person who makes the picture happen."

As you may have gathered from Bates' words, the correct answer to the question "What does a producer do?" is the same as the answer to "Where does a 500-pound gorilla sleep?" A producer does anything he wants. He hires and fires actors, hires and fires (and fires and fires) writers, oversees the director, selects the locations, chooses songs for the soundtrack... anything. Which includes, sometimes, doing nothing (which is often the wisest course of action for him to take).

It must be noted that, of late, many of the producer's functions have been usurped by studio executives. Most of these men and women hail from business backgrounds rather than the creative community, and the results of their co-opting the producer's role can largely be seen in the types of projects now emerging from the studios. Endless remakes, "reboots," sequels, films based on comic books, video games, action figures... the way things are going, *Chips Ahoy: The Movie* might be right around the corner. For these business-minded folks, it all comes down to the promotion of a brand, whether it's a product like G. I. Joe toys or a genuine creative franchise like Spider-Man or the *Halloween* movies. After all, any business school will tell you that it's far more cost-effective to simply repackage an existing property and try to resell it as something new than to roll the dice on an untested product and hope it catches on with a fickle public. Writers are constantly being told that their spec scripts, original and exciting though they may be, cannot be produced because the material has no "pre-sale value." In other words, you wrote a great script, kid, but people have heard of Chutes and Ladders, so guess which project gets the green light?

EXERCISE: WHAT IS A PRODUCER?
In brief, define your thoughts on the producer's role in screenplay development. What is the central role a producer should play in preparing a script for the screen? What do you think is a producer's most valuable input with regard to the script? What is the principal way in which the producer's perspective harms the development of a screenplay?

_____

_____

_____

_____

_____

_____

_____

_____

_____

_____

_____

Chapter Sixteen

SCREEN CREDITS,
or Joining the Desaparecidos

*. . . our imagination cannot tolerate the thought of a
state of nonexistence, the image of total negation
and extinction of our consciousness.*

— Carl Goldberg,
from *Speaking with the Devil*

———————

WRITERS ARE A MOVIE DIRECTOR'S worst nightmare.
Very few things in this world ruffle a director's feathers, but
even the flintiest helmsman wakes up in the middle of the
night drenched in a cold sweat at the thought of the existence
of *writers*. Directors fear, loathe, dread, hate writers.

This odium is because the writer's existence suggests that
the director is not the sole, cosmos-filling *auteur* behind the film
he directs, and this thought cannot be borne (by the director,
at any rate). It is the cinematic equivalent of the Freudian "pri-
mal scene," which can reduce the strongest man to a screaming
heap on the floor.

Therefore, whenever a director undertakes a new film, his
first, last, and middle priority is to *obliterate the contributions of
the writer* at all costs.

His technique is twofold. First, he either rewrites the screenplay himself or, if he is illiterate, hires his own writer to rewrite
it for him. He hires, in fact, as many writers as possible to do the
rewrites, because he knows that in the resulting proliferation of
credits, the original screenwriter's name will essentially vanish
beneath a heap of other, later names.

Then, upon completion of the film, the director will attempt to have any name *other than that of the original writer* listed in the credits as the screenplay's author. But if blind fate and the Writers Guild deny him this sleight-of-hand, he can almost always arrange for three or more writers to be credited with the film's authorship… effectively rendering all these writers invisible to both the public and the industry itself. They become the *desaparecidos*. The director feels better, and he can push this whole traumatic business out of his mind almost completely.

In Joseph McBride's 1992 biography *Frank Capra: The Catastrophe of Success*, he writes of the celebrated director:

> His basic self-doubt was multiplied by his anxiety over the fact that he had to share his success with someone else… It was a question that went to the heart of the collaborative nature of his chosen profession, and to the darkest undercurrents of doubt underlying Capra's egotism: How much did he have to do with his own success?
>
> Capra may have suffered from what would be described in 1978 by psychologists Pauline Clance and Suzanne Imes as "the impostor phenomenon," the fear common to many high achievers that their success is actually based on a fraud….
>
> In Capra's case, the need to appropriate credit belonging to his writers stemmed from his insecurity about the nature of his own abilities and achievements… he was never sure that he deserved all of that money and all of that acclaim just for sitting in a director's chair.[37]

In the *Directors Guild* magazine from July–August 1996, my old pal John Carpenter addressed the issue like this: "Let me tell you something, a screenplay is not a movie, it's a bunch of words. The director makes the movie. All this other bullshit can just go away… As a director, I am the author of my movies…

---

[37] Joseph McBride, *Frank Capra: The Catastrophe of Success* (New York: Simon & Schuster, 1992), 312–313.

If the writer thinks he's an *auteur*, then let him thread up his screenplay in a projector and we'll take a look at it."

The public happily goes along with this notion of director as "author" of the film, for it is gratifying (not to mention less confusing) to think of a film as something like a book, the product of a single mind and the sweat of a single brow. Joe Sixpack likes to imagine that the director makes it all up and then hands out assignments to his team of trolls who busy their anonymous little selves carrying out the great man's vision.

Likewise, movie reviewers (who style themselves as "critics" in much the same way that janitors refer to themselves as "industrial maintenance engineers") perpetuate this assumption with a vengeance. You would think that "critics," who are writers, after all, would be interested in promoting the interests of other writers. But this assumption overlooks the fact that most film critics hate screenwriters because they are not screenwriters themselves (or because they tried to be screenwriters and failed). So they always gleefully refer to "Fred Wilcox's *Forbidden Planet*" or "Norman Maurer's *The Three Stooges Go Around the World in a Daze.*"

And let us not forget that, to the American People, a writer is a double-dome, a freak. The idea that a writer makes up an entire movie in his head and then writes it down on paper is not only hateful, but virtually incomprehensible to a person challenged by anything longer and more complicated than a laundry list. (A member of the movie-going public once asked me, in puzzlement, "What do you do? *Write the words?*") Short of personally promoting yourself, you can't do anything about this, so you'd better get used to it.

The one thing you *can* do is join the Writers Guild. Their membership requirements are complex, but basically, if a studio starts shooting your script, you can join (and sometimes, if the studio wants the script badly enough, they will pay your first year's dues as part of your contract). You should join right away, while the film is still in production, because this association will allow you to demand credit arbitration once the picture is completed.

The way it works is like this: About the time they're wrapping up the editing process, the studio will, as required by labor contracts, send all participating writers a document entitled "Notice of Intended Writing Credits." One page in length, it will state the screenwriting credit the studio intends to put on the film, if they can get away with it. It will look like this:

Screenplay by
(Director's name)
and
(six hacks hired by Director)
Story by
(Director and six hacks) and You

At this point you should immediately contact the Writers Guild and tell it you want a credit arbitration. If you are a new member, it will stonewall and red-tape you all over the place, so you must be very insistent, and you will be granted your arbitration once it realizes that you won't be brushed off.

Now you must submit a letter to the arbitration committee, putting in writing what you think the credit should be and why. You must prepare a statement to the effect that if there is a God, only one credit is possible:

Original story and screenplay
by
You

Several weeks later, you and everyone else concerned will receive a letter, or maybe a phone call, announcing that the credit will be:

Written by
You and two hacks

And that will be that.

All the other writers will immediately appeal this decision, but they will be turned down. The director will take out full-page ads in *Variety* and *The Hollywood Reporter* denouncing you as a fraud and a thief and claiming that his pet writer was the true author of the screenplay. But by this point, it will just be sour grapes.

EXERCISE: SCREEN CREDITS
Pick up a book that discusses the production of a favorite film and review the sections regarding the writing process. Note the writers identified as having major roles in the development and final form of the screenplay, including what roles (if any) the producers, directors, and actors played in shaping the script. (If the script is an adaptation of a book, play or other property, also note input from the author of the original material.) Who received on-screen writing credit for the final film? Who, based on your research, should have received final credit?

Film _____

Writers Involved _____

_____

_____

_____

Writers Credited _____

_____

_____

_____

Who SHOULD Have Gotten Credit _____

_____

_____

_____

Chapter Seventeen

WHY BE A SCREEN WRITER?
or I'll Make This Brief

That's where the money is.

> — Willie Sutton, when asked
> why he robbed banks
> (probably apocryphal)

W HY BE A SCREENWRITER?
Because it pays well, and you can work at home.

EXERCISE: WHY BE A SCREENWRITER?
Everyone who wants to be a screenwriter has his or her unique reasons. What's yours? For your own clarification and understanding, outline exactly why you want to write screenplays. And no reason is "wrong" if it's legitimately why you want to do it. Don't hesitate to write anything here. No one will be around to check your work.

Chapter Eighteen

FEAR,
or Taking in the Garbage

Fear is only as deep as the mind allows.

— Japanese proverb

IN A WAY, THIS BOOK, an explanation of screenplay structure, is also an epitaph for the same. Story structure, at least as I learned and practice it, is going the way of the dinosaur. DVD and Blu-ray technology has made it possible to skip through a film's scenes in random order, and who's to say what a film's "real" form is when nearly every DVD features an "extended cut" or "deleted scenes"? (Has it ever occurred to anyone that maybe the reason those scenes were deleted in the first place is that the movie didn't work as well with them in there?) TiVo does the same thing to television programs that DVDs and Blu-ray do to films: They put the structure of the program being viewed in the hands of the audience, not the artwork's creator. Combine this control with interactive entertainment technology, Netflix Instant, and all the rest, and it basically makes nonsense of the theatrical viewing experience. When an audience can watch a film at home, in pieces, any time it wants; when it can enter and exit anywhere in the story; when it can jump around in a way that eliminates whole acts; when it can freeze the frame and run a film slower than normal, or faster, or backward; when it can just sit with a finger on a button and blow through channels, absorbing minute shards of story like popping M & Ms... well, all I can say is that your job and mine have become, and will continue to be, a very different thing.

So you've just read an entire book explaining a storytelling format I'm now declaring bound for extinction. Does that scare you a little bit? Good. Because ultimately, the only proper subject for art is fear. Every character in every great story ever told is motivated, at base, by fear of something. Charles Foster Kane is afraid of living his life without the love that he feels is his right. Jerry and Joe in *Some Like It Hot* are afraid of getting their heads blown off by gangsters. Norman Bates in *Psycho* is so terrified by the thought of living without his domineering mother that he mutates his own mind to keep her alive. Characters commit great and terrible acts and engage in epic struggles to conquer their fears. And people will flock to witness those struggles if the on-screen stories speak, in some fashion, to their own fears.

At the end of the day, art exists neither to instruct nor to improve, and the word "entertain" must be understood generously. True art is as wild as reality itself, and any work that is not, at bottom, about fear is not legitimate — not real art. Call it what you will: pseudo-art, non-art, even garbage art.

But there will be plenty of times in your career when you will be called upon to write work intended to both instruct *and* improve. Meanwhile, when you ask half the moviegoers in the world what they're looking for in a film, they'll say, "I just want to be entertained."

In short, the professional screenwriter must have the ability to write garbage art. But there's no reason you can't slip some truth-telling in there if you get the chance. And if you just happen to help some viewer confront his real fears, maybe even defeat them, while he's being entertained?

I won't tell if you won't.

EXERCISE: FEAR

What is your biggest fear about pursuing a career as a screen-writer? Does the idea of meeting with a producer or studio executive make your palms sweat? Are you afraid of encountering the tyrannical director types I described in Chapter Sixteen? Or is the simple sight of a blank page or white computer screen your primary nightmare fuel? Write out your biggest fear below... and how you might go about defeating it, through means described in this book or some other way.

_____

_____

_____

_____

_____

_____

_____

_____

_____

_____

_____

CONCLUSION
by Matt R. Lohr

D<small>AN</small> BEGAN WRITING THIS BOOK before he and I
ever met, and his intention in doing so was not to give me a
roundabout crash course in Writing the Dan O'Bannon Way.
Nevertheless, the process of working on this book with Dan,
and then completing it in the years A. D. (After Dan), provided
me with a thorough grounding in the art and craft of writing
for the screen, O'Bannon style. I have no way of knowing what
lessons you may have gleaned from the pages of this book, but I
can certainly share with you the things I learned while helping
Dan bring his vision to completion.

The most important lesson I gained from Dan's work is best
summed up by Jean Renoir's words from his 1939 French masterpiece *The Rules of the Game:* "Everybody has their reasons."
Many screenwriting systems I have encountered over the years,
including several of those outlined in this book, operate on the
principle of *conflict* as the narrative engine of cinematic storytelling. What is notable about most of those systems, however,
is that they choose to define the idea of story from only *one
side of the conflict.* In other words, a story is about a character who wants something, and who comes into conflict with
various aspects of his world (natural elements, personality de-
fects, other characters) as he attempts to get what he wants.
Dan was the first screenwriting instructor I came across who
was astute enough to define conflict not as *protagonist versus
obstacles*, but as *antagonists in opposition*. We know that in
Alien, Ripley, Dallas, and the rest of the ship's crew want to

survive the alien's onslaught. Dan's inspiration was to consider the flip side of that question: "What does the alien want?" In this case, it's to survive at all costs, and if he has to tear, chew, and acid-burn his way through a gang of innocent humans to do so, tough break for them. Dan's films are notable for featuring strong "negative antagonists," characters with criminal or malevolent goals, in opposition to "positive antagonists" whose goals more closely reflect the finer leanings of life. In most screenwriting structural systems, these latter characters would be referred to as "protagonists," and the story would be defined entirely in terms of *their* struggle. But Dan always made sure that the negative antagonists' goals were as sharply etched and readily understandable as those of his ostensible protagonists; the conflicts presented were well-rounded ones, with motivations, actions, and reactions clearly defined on both sides of the firing line. Film critics are fond of asserting that the best villains are often those who are the most relatable to the viewer; characters operating from motivations that, even if we don't share them, at least make some sort of sense to us. Though I wouldn't agree that this clarity is always the case (surely the Joker in *The Dark Knight* ranks as an all-time cinematic villain, but he tells us himself that his actions spring from motivations that even he doesn't comprehend), it's a solid principle for structuring your screenplay's conflict, and Dan's system takes that principle as its guiding philosophy. Everybody has his reasons, and if you can make your audience understand those reasons, no matter the moral or legal consequences, you are on your way to crafting a solid cinematic experience.

Another important take-away from the experience of writing this book was Dan's lack of snobbery. The preceding pages clearly reflect a considerable intellect, a man at home with the words and ideas of the greatest philosophers and wits of the ages. And yet, he plied his trade and consolidated his legend by creating the kinds of pictures that many self-defined *cineastes* would turn up their noses at: alien-invasion epics, high-tech action flicks, zombie thrillers, and adaptations of the work of H. P. Lovecraft, a man regarded by some as "American literature's greatest bad writer."[38] But Dan was a writer who never wrote down to the public perception of his chosen genres. To him, *Alien* was not "only" a science fiction thriller, *The Return of the Living Dead* not "just" a zombie movie. He gave as much care and consideration to these films as would any artist who truly believes in the value of the work he's putting forth. This passionate belief in the value of his efforts sometimes led Dan to butt heads with those whose grand visions for the films in question extended no further than their pecuniary potential. But this reality only served to remind me of one of the most important lessons any artist, in any medium, can learn: In creating a work of art, theme and subject are less important than skill and ingenuity of execution. There's no such thing as an unworthy subject for a film, if you approach it with sincerity and give it your best creative effort. If you're writing a quickie direct-to-video creature feature to be dumped in Redbox machines nationwide, you owe it to your muse (not to mention your audience) to create the best damn quickie monster flick you and the budget can muster up. Better to write quality "trash" that you really believe in, than to spend your days creating "high art" that leaves you bored and your audience unfulfilled.

Most of my own work on the initial draft of this manuscript was done on Chapter Seven, in which Dan's system is put to the test against a raft of stage and screen works, both unassailable masterpieces and more problematic texts. The results cemented the third major lesson I took away from working with Dan. The ideas and concepts that make up Dan's system may be unique to both his process and this book, but the proof of their value can be found in centuries' worth of storytelling tradition. Filmmakers Dan never met, indeed who were plying their trade before he was even born, were making effective use

---

[38] Laura Miller, "Master of Disgust," Salon.com, February 12, 2005, retrieved from http://www.salon.com/2005/02/12/lovecraft/

of principles analogous to those inherent to Dan's system (and, in the case of *Dracula* and *Lost Horizon*, misusing those same principles, to the detriment of those films.) What's more, the bedrock ideas behind dynamic structure predate cinema entirely. As we've illustrated, Shakespeare and Ibsen both utilized the same storytelling techniques that drive Dan's work, and though the scope of our analyses doesn't extend all the way back to the dawn of stage drama, one suspects that in examining the works of the great ancient playwrights, the presence of basic storytelling principles very similar to Dan's would likely be uncovered. (Oedipus putting out his eyes upon learning what he's done to his parents sure seems like a Point of No Return, doesn't it? Shakespeare might think so. After all, in *King Lear*, what was The Point of No Return? A character getting his eyes gouged out.) Dan's system was proprietary, and he arrived at it through studious trial and error, but at its heart lies a concept of story structure that has formed the basis for the entire canon of Western drama. If using Dan's system results in a story that you perceive to be incorrect in its structural undergirding, you may want to hop in your Wayback Machine and go gripe to Shakespeare and Ibsen, because according to you, they've got it wrong, too.

DAN AND I HAVE KEPT THIS BOOK fairly firmly focused on the structural aspects of screenwriting. If you picked up this volume hoping to learn how to write memorable dialogue, craft the perfect action set-piece, or hook your reader in the first ten pages, I'm sorry — you came to the wrong place. Likewise, if you were looking for a book to guide you through the treacherous shoals of the screenwriting *business*, to help you land an agent, make a big sale, and rake in Dan O'Bannon–sized box office returns, I again apologize if the preceding couple hundred pages weren't exactly what you were after.

But if your story is a mess, if your conflict isn't properly set up and doesn't build to an appropriate Point of No Return that solidly pays off in Act Three, all the catchy lines and rev-'em-up kaboom moments in the world aren't going to help you write a script that works. And artistic shortcomings will inevitably be followed by commercial setbacks. In other words, if the script doesn't compel, it doesn't sell. So, in this book, you may not have found all the information you're looking for in your quest to create the best screenplay you can write — but you've found the *first* information you need, and to paraphrase the words of another great writer (a lyricist, not a screenwriter), starting at the very beginning is, indeed, a very good place to start.

My sincerest wish is that Dan's system, and the success of the masterworks that he created by applying it, will serve as instruction and inspiration as you tackle your own screenwriting projects. I'm rooting for you. And though Dan was not anyone's idea of a sentimental slob, wherever he is now, I know he's cheering you on, too.

AFTERWORD
by Diane O'Bannon

WHEN DAN FINISHED THE MANUSCRIPT for this book, he gave it to me to read. He said, "I haven't put in the part about hedonic adaptation. I can't tell every secret, you know." He thought the concept of hedonic adaptation was so valuable he was going to keep it for himself. Because he is gone now, I have decided to put it in.

My deep thanks to Michael Wiese and his able associate, Ken Lee, for finding Dan's book and bringing it to its intended audience. Michael Wiese Productions must be unique in being businesslike while remaining spiritually alive to its writers and their intent.

My heartfelt thanks to Matt Lohr for bringing this book to fruition. His dedication to this project and his writing talent have made it possible for Dan's insights and experience to be brought to the reader. This book could not have gone forward without him.

~ *Diane O'Bannon*
   January 25, 2012

DAN O'BANNON:
A Filmography

Dan O'Bannon receives screen credit on the following films...

* *Dark Star* (1974): Original story and screenplay (with John Carpenter); special effects supervisor; editor; production designer; actor (as Sgt. Pinback)

* *Star Wars* (1977): Computer animation and graphic displays; miniature and optical effects unit

* *Alien* (1979): Story (with Ronald Shusett); screenplay; visual design consultant

* *Dead and Buried* (1981): Screenplay (with Ronald Shusett)

* *Heavy Metal* (1981): Original story, "Soft Landing" segment; story, "B-17" segment

* *Blue Thunder* (1983): Original story and screenplay (with Don Jakoby)

* *Blue Thunder* TV series (1984): Executive story consultant; story, "The Island" episode; story/teleplay, "Arms Race" episode

* *The Return of the Living Dead* (1985): Screenplay; director

* *Lifeforce* (1985): Screenplay (with Don Jakoby)

* *Invaders From Mars* (1986): Screenplay (with Don Jakoby)

* *Aliens* (1986): Character creator

* *Total Recall* (1990): Screen story (with Ronald Shusett & Dan O'Bannon and Gary Goldman); screenplay (with Ronald Shusett & Dan O'Bannon and Jon Povill)

* *Alien 3* (1992): Character creator

* *The Resurrected*, a.k.a. *Shatterbrain* (1992): Director

* *Screamers* (1995): Screenplay (with Miguel Tejada-Flores)

* *Bleeders* (1997): Screenplay (with Charles Adair and Ronald Shusett)

* *Alien: Resurrection* (1997): Character creator

* *Delivering Milo* (2001): Actor (as Clerk)

* *AVP: Alien Vs. Predator* (2004): Alien character creator; screen story (with Paul W.S. Anderson and Ronald Shusett)

* *AVPR: Alien Vs. Predator – Requiem* (2007): Alien character creator

ABOUT THE AUTHORS

DAN O'BANNON was born in Missouri in 1946. He was a scholarship student in fine arts at Washington University in St. Louis before moving to Los Angeles in 1969 to study film at the University of Southern California. While at USC, he collaborated with John Carpenter on the screenplay for what would become Dan's first feature film, 1974's *Dark Star*, in which he also costarred as "Sgt. Pinback."

Photo by Barry Slobin

Dan's credits include eleven produced screenplays, largely in the science fiction and horror genres. He is best known for his work on the Oscar-winning international blockbuster *Alien*, which ranked as number 6 on the American Film Institute's countdown of the 100 most thrilling American films; in 2002, this picture was inducted into the Library of Congress' National Film Registry. Dan's other credits include the Arnold Schwarzenegger hit *Total Recall, Blue Thunder,* and *Screamers*. Dan also directed two feature films, *The Return of the Living Dead* (which he also wrote) and *The Resurrected*. He taught film studies and writing courses at USC and at Chapman University in Orange, CA.

Dan's later years were spent with his wife, Diane, and son in Los Angeles. He died of complications from Crohn's disease in 2009.

ABOUT THE AUTHORS

A native of Pittsburgh, PA, MATT R. LOHR is an award-winning screenwriter, essayist, and critic. He holds an MFA in screenwriting from Chapman University in Orange, CA, where he first met Dan O'Bannon and agreed to work with him on this book. His views on contemporary and classic cinema can be found on his blog, "The Movie Zombie" (*themoviezombie. blogspot.com*).

Photo by Zack Whitford

Matt is also the host of the forthcoming Dan O'Bannon Writing Workshops,™ which will bring a hands-on presentation of Dan's "dynamic structure" screenplay system to seminars, pitchfests, and industry events worldwide. More information on these events, and on all upcoming projects and programs relating to Dan's works and teaching, is available online at the official Dan O'Bannon website, www.danobannon.com. Matt can be contacted by email at matt@danobannon.com, and he is available on Twitter by following @DanOBannonBook.

Matt currently lives in Los Angeles.

About the Authors

Photo by Jewel Shepard

DIANE O'BANNON met her future husband Dan at USC, while he was in preproduction on *Dark Star*. Following a years-long, on-again off-again connection, Diane and Dan married in 1986, a union that lasted until his death in 2009.

Diane continues to shepherd unproduced and unpublished Dan O'Bannon works into the wider world. She is currently preparing a publication of Dan's own version of the *Necronomicon*, and is in negotiations regarding posthumous production of several of his screenplays. Additional information on these projects and others can be found on the Dan O'Bannon website, and on Dan's official fan page on Facebook. Inquiries can be directed to Diane at diane@danobannon.com.

Diane lives in Los Angeles with her son, Adam.

THE MYTH OF MWP

In a dark time, a light bringer came along, leading the curious and the frustrated to clarity and empowerment. It took the well-guarded secrets out of the hands of the few and made them available to all. It spread a spirit of openness and creative freedom, and built a storehouse of knowledge dedicated to the betterment of the arts.

The essence of the Michael Wiese Productions (MWP) is empowering people who have the burning desire to express themselves creatively. We help them realize their dreams by putting the tools in their hands. We demystify the sometimes secretive worlds of screenwriting, directing, acting, producing, film financing, and other media crafts.

By doing so, we hope to bring forth a realization of 'conscious media' which we define as being positively charged, emphasizing hope and affirming positive values like trust, cooperation, self-empowerment, freedom, and love. Grounded in the deep roots of myth, it aims to be healing both for those who make the art and those who encounter it. It hopes to be transformative for people, opening doors to new possibilities and pulling back veils to reveal hidden worlds.

MWP has built a storehouse of knowledge unequaled in the world, for no other publisher has so many titles on the media arts. Please visit www.mwp.com where you will find many free resources and a 25% discount on our books. Sign up and become part of the wider creative community!

Onward and upward,

Michael Wiese
Publisher/Filmmaker

THE WRITER'S JOURNEY – 3RD EDITION
MYTHIC STRUCTURE FOR WRITERS

CHRISTOPHER VOGLER

BEST SELLER

See why this book has become an international best seller and a true classic. *The Writer's Journey* explores the powerful relationship between mythology and storytelling in a clear, concise style that's made it required reading for movie executives, screenwriters, playwrights, scholars, and fans of pop culture all over the world.

Both fiction and nonfiction writers will discover a set of useful myth-inspired storytelling paradigms (i.e., "The Hero's Journey") and step-by-step guidelines to plot and character development. Based on the work of Joseph Campbell, *The Writer's Journey* is a must for all writers interested in further developing their craft.

The updated and revised third edition provides new insights and observations from Vogler's ongoing work on mythology's influence on stories, movies, and man himself.

"This book is like having the smartest person in the story meeting come home with you and whisper what to do in your ear as you write a screenplay. Insight for insight, step for step, Chris Vogler takes us through the process of connecting theme to story and making a script come alive."
> – Lynda Obst, producer, *Sleepless in Seattle, How to Lose a Guy in 10 Days*;
> author, *Hello, He Lied*

"This is a book about the stories we write, and perhaps more importantly, the stories we live. It is the most influential work I have yet encountered on the art, nature, and the very purpose of storytelling."
> – Bruce Joel Rubin, screenwriter, *Stuart Little 2, Deep Impact,*
> *Ghost, Jacob's Ladder*

CHRISTOPHER VOGLER is a veteran story consultant for major Hollywood film companies and a respected teacher of filmmakers and writers around the globe. He has influenced the stories of movies from *The Lion King* to *Fight Club* to *The Thin Red Line* and most recently wrote the first installment of *Ravenskull*, a Japanese-style manga or graphic novel. He is the executive producer of the feature film *P. S. Your Cat is Dead* and writer of the animated feature *Jester Till*.

$26.95 · 448 PAGES · ORDER NUMBER 76RLS · ISBN: 9781932907360

SAVE THE CAT!.
THE LAST BOOK ON SCREENWRITING YOU'LL EVER NEED!

BLAKE SNYDER

BEST SELLER

BLAKE SNYDER

He made millions of dollars selling screenplays to Hollywood and here screenwriter Blake Snyder tells all. "Save the Cat!." is just one of Snyder's many ironclad rules for making your ideas more marketable and your script more satisfying — and saleable, including:

- The four elements of every winning logline.
- The seven immutable laws of screenplay physics.
- The 10 genres and why they're important to your movie.
- Why your Hero must serve your idea.
- Mastering the Beats.
- Mastering the Board to create the Perfect Beast.
- How to get back on track with ironclad and proven rules for script repair.

This ultimate insider's guide reveals the secrets that none dare admit, told by a show biz veteran who's proven that you can sell your script if you can save the cat.

"Imagine what would happen in a town where more writers approached screenwriting the way Blake suggests? My weekend read would dramatically improve, both in sellable/producible content and in discovering new writers who understand the craft of storytelling and can be hired on assignment for ideas we already have in house."

> – From the Foreword by Sheila Hanahan Taylor, Vice President, Development at Zide/Perry Entertainment, whose films include *American Pie, Cats and Dogs, Final Destination*

"One of the most comprehensive and insightful how-to's out there. Save the Cat!. *is a must-read for both the novice and the professional screenwriter."*

> – Todd Black, Producer, *The Pursuit of Happyness, The Weather Man, S.W.A.T, Alex and Emma, Antwone Fisher*

"Want to know how to be a successful writer in Hollywood? The answers are here. Blake Snyder has written an insider's book that's informative — and funny, too."

> – David Hoberman, Producer, *The Shaggy Dog* (2005), *Raising Helen, Walking Tall, Bringing Down the House, Monk* (TV)

BLAKE SNYDER, besides selling million-dollar scripts to both Disney and Spielberg, was one of Hollywood's most successful spec screenwriters. Blake's vision continues on *www.blakesnyder.com*.

$19.95 · 216 PAGES · ORDER NUMBER 34RLS · ISBN: 9781932907001

CPSIA information can be obtained
at www.ICGtesting.com
Printed in the USA
JSHW011327120820
7265JS00002B/49